The big book *of* virtual team-building games

The big book of virtual team-building games

Quick, effective activities to build communication, trust, and collaboration from anywhere!

Mary Scannell, Michael Abrams & Mike Mulvihill

New York Chicago San Francisco Lisbon London Madrid Mexico City
Milan New Delhi San Juan Seoul Singapore Sydney Toronto

The McGraw-Hill Companies

1 2 3 4 5 6 7 8 9 10 QFR/QFR 1 9 8 7 6 5 4 3 2 1

ISBN 978-0-07-177435-2
MHID 0-07-177435-1

e-ISBN 978-0-07-177512-0
e-MHID 0-07-177512-9

Library of Congress Cataloging-in-Publication Data

Scannell, Mary, date
Big book of virtual team-building games : quick, effective activities to build communication, trust and collaboration from anywhere! / by Mary Scannell, Michael Abrams, Mike Mulvihill. — 1st ed.
p. cm.
ISBN-13: 978-0-07-177435-2 (alk. paper)
ISBN-10: 0-07-177435-1 (alk. paper)
1. Teams in the workplace. 2. Group games. 3. Management games.
I. Abrams, Michael. II. Mulvihill, Mike. III. Title.

HD66.S23 2012
658.4'022—dc23

2011037657

This book is printed on acid-free paper.

Contents

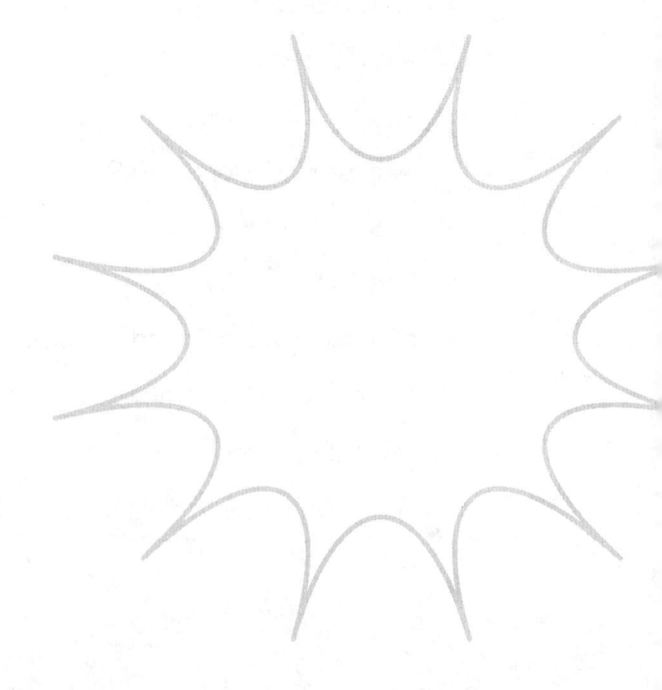

Acknowledgments

A big thank-you to Edward E. Scannell and Dr. John Newstrom for originating the Big Books; we are honored to contribute to the series.

To MaryTherese Church and Donya Dickerson, our editors at McGraw-Hill, thank you for the opportunity to take this idea and run with it. We appreciated the energy you shared with us to get it started. Thanks to Julia Baxter, our marketing and promotion guru at McGraw-Hill, for your hard work and dedication while promoting the book. To Rena Copperman and her team, including Carolyn Wendt, thank you for your eye for detail during the editing and production process.

Our heartfelt appreciation goes out to all our workshop attendees, our teambuilding participants, and our clients. You guided us to this project, and this book is for you. You taught us that we all need meaningful connections, whether we work on a traditional or a virtual team. Thank you for the opportunity to work with you.

And on a personal note:

A sincere thank-you to my dad, Ed, for your optimism, enthusiasm, and support. I am so lucky that you are my number one fan and the person who I can always count on for love and guidance. Above all, thank you for passing on your passion for training and development and your love of games.

— Mary Scannell

I would like to give my family a great big hug for all their support and energy in making this book happen. I'm also very grateful to all the leaders and teams I've had the honor of working with over the years who have helped develop and challenge me to do and be more. Finally, a big shoutout to B&B Bagels on Long Island, New York, for teaching me what it really means to work as a team. My fingers have nearly healed.

— Michael T. Abrams

I would like to thank my wife, Chrissy, for her love and support during the writing of this book. Thanks also to my family—Bob and Mary Mulvihill, Anna Farrier, and Patrick Mulvihill— for the countless ways they've guided me, encouraged me, and cheered for me throughout the years.

— Mike Mulvihill

The big book *of* virtual team-building games

What Is a Virtual Team, Anyway?

A virtual team is a team that is *separated* by distance, time, or both, and *connected* by purpose and technology.

The Benefit of Virtual Teams

Virtual teams allow organizations to be more flexible. Technology connects leaders and innovators around the globe, reduces travel time, and enables rapid decision making through nearly instantaneous communication. With rapidly advancing technology and increasing globalization, virtual teams are here to stay.

A virtual team has the luxury of securing the best individuals for the team, no matter where they are located. A virtual team can provide around-the-clock coverage, enabling the organization to respond to customers at any time. Introverted or shy team members often thrive in a virtual team that provides them isolated and focused work time and also time to contemplate before answering an email. Virtual teams can also be more diverse, in that language barriers can be overcome through the technologies used by a virtual team. In addition, team members with physical limitations that may prevent them from participating in "real-life" team-building activities can contribute. Having no commute or travel time can add up to greater productivity. Many virtual team members discover that they not only experience greater productivity, but also a better work–life balance.

The Challenges of Working Virtually

While technology is advancing, there are, however, challenges to working across physical and cultural divides. Just like traditional teams, virtual teams experience all the stages of group formation: Forming, Storming, Norming, Performing, and Transforming; but at a different pace. Our ability to communicate and connect can enhance or diminish the purpose and potential of virtual teaming. Because the nonverbal component is lost, communication and trust are typically not at the same level virtually as in face-to-face interactions. There are no lively water-cooler debates and discussions that help form solid relationships. In the absence of solid relationships, virtual team members have a tendency toward quick agreement, which may sound like a good thing, but in the long run does the team a great disservice when it comes to the team members' ability to brainstorm, problem- solve, and navigate through conflict.

Certain rules of behavior that are taken for granted in person have to be given special care in virtual teams. For example, during an in-person meeting, some great ideas come about during the breaks or downtime. In the virtual world, there is no lingering after meetings to decompress, contemplate, and connect. This is the informal coming together that has to be formally planned in the virtual world.

Usually the first time these challenges are discovered is after the damage has been done. Consistent training and specifically team building in the forming stage of group development can develop trust and foster more effective communication. This deeper level of trust and communication leads to cohesiveness, commitment to team goals, and better and faster decisions.

How to Overcome the Challenges of Working Virtually

When your team is *separated* by distance and time, meet the challenge with communication, trust, and technology.

To ensure your team stays *connected* by purpose and technology, create a clear vision and understanding of team goals; why team members were chosen to be on the team; correct use of technology; and team members' knowledge of, and ability to use, diverse technology.

Developing an effective virtual team requires the same techniques as developing an effective traditional team. Teams experience forming, storming, norming, performing, and transforming. The main difference is the time it takes to progress through the stages, especially the first two stages. On a traditional team, relationships and trust are built during the unplanned moments throughout the day. Watercooler discussions, informal chats in the break room, and hallway conversations allow team members to get to know each other in a relaxed and casual manner. Through these interpersonal interactions, trust develops naturally over time. Because the virtual team does not operate in the same manner, many of these impromptu conversations and connections have to be planned for and built into team conference calls or other types of team meetings. That is where the activities in this book can help. These games and activities provide tools to build a strong team foundation by developing trusting relationships, communicating effectively, and using technology to enhance the team's connections.

Goal

The goal of anyone who leads a virtual team is to ensure that the *only* thing that separates members of your team is distance and time. The first and most important way to bring your team together is through a shared purpose. What is the purpose of your virtual team and why were the team members chosen to be on the team?

Norms, Rituals, and Operating Agreements

Create a level of comfort within the team and build consistency by creating team norms, rituals, and operating agreements. These are the rules and codes of conduct the team members agree to comply with and operate under. Team norms and operating agreements reduce conflict within the team and make it easier for team members to hold each other accountable.

Post the norms and operating agreements in a prominent place, such as a team website or web book. Posting also ensures the team has access to this information at any time and gives new members a better understanding of what is expected. New team members can be more easily assimilated into the team if, during the introduction process, an established team member takes the new person through the norms and operating agreements to explain why each one is important and ways to best apply them.

Norms

Norms relate to how team members normally conduct themselves. Norms and rituals are essential for a virtual team. When team members have a hand in creating their team's norms and rituals, there is a higher level of accountability and commitment to the norms. Creating and posting positive team norms solidifies the importance of adhering to the norms.

Some examples of positive team norms

- Assuming team members are trustworthy
- Listening *for* rather than *in judgment of* the other person
- Reading email *for* rather than *against* the other person
- Adopting a "yes, and" rather than a "yes, but" feedback style
- One person speaking at a time
- Voicing opinions during, not after, meetings
- Tracking and posting action items

Rituals

Rituals create the team culture and make us feel more connected to one another. Once we establish rewarding team rituals, the team sees them as "the way we do things." Rituals create a comfort zone and provide consistency and a common bond. The most effective rituals are not forced; they are comfortable, natural, and most importantly, consistent.

Some examples of team rituals

- Beginning meetings with a relationship-building game such as Entrance Music (page 191)
- Ending meetings with End on a High Note (page 145)
- Posting regular updates on the team website
- Celebrating birthdays
- Incorporating one goofy joke into every meeting
- Ending all team-related email communication with the team name, motto, or slogan

Operating Agreements

Operating agreements are similar to norms and rituals but are more structured and work-specific. Agreeing to and adhering to the team's operating agreements creates consistency and trust.

Some examples of elements of virtual team operating agreements

- Meetings—structure, agendas, length, frequency
- Decisions—how they will be made, how they will be communicated
- Communication—how to ensure everyone is informed, how to acknowledge receipt of information, how to relay bad news, how to provide feedback, how to request assistance, how confidential information is handled
- Accountability—holding ourselves and others accountable regarding deadlines and tasks
- Awareness—how to be aware of others on the team, willingness to ask for help
- Recognition—how to acknowledge other team members, how to celebrate the accomplishments of the team

Communication

Many methods of communication are available to a virtual team. Establishing protocols early will help team members choose the best technology to increase the level of communication and understanding within the team. Create opportunities for team members to gain skills and increase their comfort level with the modes of communication that will best serve the team.

Trust

For virtual teams, trust can be difficult to cultivate. One technique that helps is team members' assumption that the people on the team are trustworthy. To assist this team attitude, start with credibility. In a virtual team, you may find the first element that allows you to build trust is credibility. To establish the credibility of your team, make sure team members understand the qualifications of the other team members and why they were chosen for your team. To promote credibility, allow different team members to take leadership roles in planning and running team meetings. Having team members choose and facilitate a game from this book is a great way to get this started.

In face-to-face relationships, the first element of trust is usually our knowledge of the other person. Trust is often extended when we feel comfortable with another person, when we have an understanding of who that person is. When we share the same space with another person, we get to observe who that person is through his or her actions and words—both verbal and nonverbal communication. We naturally get a sense of another person as we interact with that person casually throughout our day. A virtual team does not operate in this same manner. The casual connections we make in person have to be planned for on your virtual team. Allowing time for these types of connections can open the door to increased trust on your virtual team.

Another component of trust is reliability. Reliability is demonstrated by consistency and dependability. Working on a team separated by time can create challenges when it comes to dependability. One team member's interpretation of another team member's reliability may not only be impacted by a time element, but also by their choice of technology and their knowledge of and comfort with technology. Many of the games in this book are designed to improve your team's skills regarding diverse technology methods so they can choose and use the best technology to fit the situation.

Technology

To overcome the challenges of being separated by distance and time, increase team members' level of trust with one another and their knowledge of technology to allow them to communicate effectively. Technology can enhance or destroy connections. First, make sure the technology is up to the job. Slow connections, dropped calls, and inadequate equipment can add up to frustration and anger for team members. Second, make sure your team members have the necessary skills and are comfortable using the different types of technology they will have available to them. In addition, provide training to help them choose the best technology for the situation. Third, establishing ground rules or team norms regarding team communication will create consistency within your team.

Best Use of Face Time

If your virtual team has the opportunity to meet face to face, it's best to get together as close to the team's inception as possible. Build into these meetings some facilitated team-building initiatives to break the ice, build trust, and develop communication skills. Allow time for casual interactions too, so your team can get to know each other better.

To make the most of an initial in-person meeting, follow these guidelines:

- Begin with informal socializing. Allow the team to mingle and engage in small talk.
- Facilitate an icebreaker that serves to create even more connections, especially for the people on your team who may be more introverted.
- The goal of this time is to promote one-on-one interactions between everyone on the team.

Some of the games in this book can be used in this scenario. Bring the team together for a trust-building activity. Choose a game that deepens the level of personal knowledge of the other team members. What's in a Name? (page 79) is an excellent choice for this. For another option, in the "Climate Setting" and "Trust" chapters of *The Big Book of Team-Motivating Games,* you will find several games that will deepen the team members' connections to each other and their team.

After that, you are ready to develop some team norms. Chances are, everyone on your team has participated in other virtual teams. What worked; what didn't? Empower the team to create norms regarding communication (phone, email, instant or text messaging, listening, multitasking during meetings), technology, response time, dealing with conflict, and so forth. The game Communication Best Practices (page 95) is a good place to begin. Also, how will we hold our teammates and ourselves accountable for upholding the norms?

Now that you have done some climate setting and problem solving (developing team norms), continue your meeting by moving on to more work-specific items.

What is the purpose for the virtual team? Consider making formal introductions here as well. Why were the people in this room chosen for the team? What background and experience does each person bring? To continue the relationship building, have team members interview one another and introduce each other to the team.

Create clear vision regarding your purpose, vision, mission, and goals. By doing this in person you will save your team countless conference calls and lay the foundation for a closer and more trusting team.

Meeting in person twice a year is ideal for a virtual team. For future in-person meetings, continue to allow plenty of time for informal interactions and to facilitate team-building activities. For example, during your second face-to-face meeting, introduce a game that incites conflict. You will find many games that serve this purpose in *The Big Book of Conflict-Resolution Games.* This, in addition to work-related items, will ensure a good balance and help team members maintain better communication when they go back to their individual locations.

Virtual Team Meetings

Establish meeting ground rules during the norming stage and stick to them. Rituals also help create consistency, establish trust, and increase the level of comfort in the virtual process.

In general, you can increase the level of engagement for your virtual team meetings by:

- Following an agenda
- Sending the agenda prior to the meeting
- Looking for ways to incorporate small discussion groups (the fewer the number of participants, the more involved individuals will be in the discussion, so look for ways to incorporate small discussion groups)
- Keeping the meeting short, concise, and lively
- Using visuals when possible

- Beginning with a game or activity that promotes personal interactions, either with a "pair and share" or with an activity for the entire team
- Supplementing the conference call with an online collaboration tool
- Passing the leadership role to others on the team
- Making sure that all technology is working properly and that the participants can access any necessary tools
- Making sure that all team members understand their roles and responsibilities for the meeting (such as scribe, presenter, leader, facilitator, and so on)
- Scheduling a short break halfway through the meeting (ten minutes should be enough, so that you don't lose momentum)
- Having everyone stay off mute when on a conference call, to eliminate multitasking and increase discussion
- Using a method for ensuring everyone's participation (such as the "clock" method [page 38], where you jot down names in the hour positions on the face of a clock and periodically go around the clock, picking a person's name starting at any position and proceeding in either direction)
- Sticking to your agenda (use a "parking lot" for off-topic ideas that can be addressed in future meetings)
- Including follow-up procedures as part of the team meeting norms—make sure the next step or follow-up is clear to the team
- Posting meeting notes on a team website, along with the follow-up agreed upon

Summary

A virtual team is similar to a traditional team in that the team is brought together by a shared purpose. Creating a clear vision of the team's purpose and goals, and a clear understanding of why the team members were chosen, helps your virtual team to begin to establish trust.

A virtual team is different from a traditional team in that team members are separated by distance and time. Differences, personalities, conflict, work styles, and communication issues can all serve to separate teams, whether conventional or virtual. Make it your goal that the only thing that separates members of your virtual team is distance and time. Make the best use of technology to create an environment where solid connections and clear communication are the norm.

Stages of Team Development

Forming
Storming Performing
Transforming
Norming

Assessing Your Team's Development

Understanding the stages of team development sets up the foundation of aligning the work of your team to their ability to do that kind of work. If you have a team that is just in the forming stage, you may not have much success in openly debating a set of potential solutions. Likewise, having a high-performing team stop and do introductions or "getting to know you" activities may bore them. High-performing teams are ready for greater and more complex challenges. Your team can only do the kind of work that they are ready to do. Each team goes through the stages differently, but the characteristics of each of the stages are fairly clear to identify. Once you are able to identify these characteristics, you will be able to assess the team's stage of development. With the stage of development identified, you can keep the expected outcomes of virtual team meetings aligned with the team's ability to achieve that kind of work.

Getting It Right

In assessing the development stage of your team you have one goal, which is to match the activities of the team to the development stage of the team. So as leaders, we are either matching or mismatching our activities to the team. That's it? Seems simple, right? No, not at all. The impact of mismatching will be felt not only by you the leader, but also by the team. Teams get frustrated when they are being asked to do things that they are not prepared to do. Let's take a look at the indicators of a match or mismatch.

Indicators of a Match

When you have properly matched the kind of work you are asking the team to do to the team's current development stage, you may see the following behaviors:

- Greater team participation and engagement
- A greater likelihood of your desired outcomes being achieved
- Team members' perception that team meetings are a valuable use of time

Indicators of a Mismatch

When you have improperly matched the kind of work you are asking the team to do to the team's current development stage, you may see the following behaviors:

- Failure to arrive on time
- High absenteeism on calls
- Lack of discussion

- Lack of commitment to deliverables
- Confusion about the purpose of meeting activities
- Team members outright challenging the need for more meetings

How many times have you attended a meeting and felt some of the indicators of a mismatch listed above? Imagine the impact of those indicators on a virtual team. As the leader of a virtual team, you may be causing these mismatch behaviors without even knowing it. The games in this book will be helpful for you to move your team through the development stages, but you must know which stage your team is in to properly align the game to the need. Let's take a look at the various ways you can assess your team's current stage of development.

Methods of Team Assessment

There are many formal and informal methods to assess your team's stage of development. There are many companies or independent consultants who will assess your team's development stage for you (for a fee, of course). For some groups, this formal consulting effort may be exactly what is needed. Most virtual teams you lead won't need this level of formality—especially since teams do not move through the stages in a linear fashion but rather more of a spiral. A team moves forward and backward through the stages as circumstances change. Adding or removing team members, changing the purpose of the team, reducing the frequency of meetings, and a change of leadership can all impact the team's development stage. These factors may accelerate a team's development or cause it to slide backward as members regroup around the change. Because of this, we recommend using the following three assessment methods to analyze your team: using a survey, active listening, and observing behaviors. They are cost effective, easy to implement, and convenient to use several times during the life span of a team.

Using a Survey

A survey is a great, quick way to assess your team's most likely stage of development. This survey is also available online at virtualteambuilding games.com. While not an exact science, it can help to provide you with a good indication of the type of team activities that would be more productive than others. To use this survey, you would poll the team members individually and anonymously to gather their responses. Do not try to have team members state their responses in front of the entire group, as this is only possible with a team in a later stage of development. Early-stage teams may not respond honestly to this survey in a public forum, thus skewing your results.

Again, this is just an indicator of the development stage of your team. This method is quick and useful to quantify your team's feelings. In addition to this survey, take the behaviors of the team into account to determine your final decision on the team's development stage.

Active Listening

Rather than use a survey, you may choose to base your understanding of the team's stage of development more on the direct interactions of team members. Active listening is simply the process of listening with intent and purpose. You are not listening for content but rather for delivery. You can practice active listening without your team even being aware you are doing this, which makes it even more flexible than using a survey. Most of us use active listening without even knowing it. For the purposes of identifying your team's stage of development, you will be actively listening for three things: what they say, how they say it, and when silence comes.

First, *what* your team says will be your first indication. Ask yourself the following questions during your next team meeting, answering yes or no:

- Do team members use positive language when interacting with each other?
- Do team members sigh or make sounds while someone else is speaking?

GET IT ONLINE!

Survey

For each of the following statements, rate your level of agreement or disagreement.

1 = *disagree*, **2** = *undecided*, **3** = *agree*

1. I clearly understand the goals and purpose of my team.
2. I understand my role on this team and the role of my fellow team members.
3. I am able to openly disagree with another team member's ideas in order to find a better solution.
4. I am able to openly debate with another team member about an idea I have submitted.
5. I clearly understand the meeting rules and guidelines our team has developed to govern how we work together.
6. Our team members regularly follow the meeting rules and guidelines we have set forth.
7. Our team is able to successfully complete tasks we have been assigned.
8. I am able to ask for help when I am in danger of failing on an assignment.
9. Our team takes time to celebrate successes and recognize the contribution of members at the completion of a project.
10. Our team is able to successfully orient new team members and continue performing at a high level with little interruption.

Once you have collected all the responses, you can score the quiz. First, ensure you have responses to each question. Missing responses will skew the final assessment results. Second, add up all the scores and divide by the total number of people who completed the survey. Third, use the following scoring chart as a guide to indicate which stage your team may be in.

Score	Scoring Chart for Development Stage of Team Assessment
10–14	Forming
15–18	Storming
19–22	Norming
23–26	Performing
27–30	Transforming

- Do team members respond when someone asks the group a question or are they quiet for extended periods of time?
- When team members have joined a conference call early, do they interact with each other or is the call silent until the leader joins?
- Do team members ask questions to gain clarity?
- Do team members sound defensive when they are debating a point?
- Do team members laugh at appropriate times?
- Do team members introduce and greet each other as they join the call?
- Do team members say good-bye when they leave the call?
- Do team members identify themselves when they join the call late?

Count the number of yes and no responses you came up with. The more yes responses you have would indicate the more mature or developed your team may be. A large number of no responses would indicate you have a team that is still struggling with the core stages of development. You cannot have a high-performing team that demonstrates the behaviors of a forming- or storming-stage team. The skills of the forming and storming stages are prerequisites for the high-performing stage. You cannot successfully skip a stage and expect long-term success. Eventually, those chickens come home to roost.

You will need to determine your own comfort level with the number of no responses you gave. Select the chapter in this book that most closely aligns with your team's stage of development.

Observing Behaviors

The last method we recommend using is the practice of observing the behaviors of your team. This is the most common method of identifying the development stage of your team. Members of teams must work together to achieve their goal. In the work of getting to that goal, there are observable behaviors your team will demonstrate. This method is great to use due to its flexibility, ease of use, and the reality that behaviors are a manifestation of how people really work together.

For each of the five stages of development, we have identified some key behaviors you should see your team demonstrating. Keep in mind each of the stages builds on the stages that precede it. So in stage three, your team is still modeling behaviors of stages one and two. If you find certain behaviors your team is not demonstrating, first determine if the tasks they perform are providing them an opportunity to demonstrate these behaviors. For instance, if your team never needs to brainstorm ideas, then it would be unfair to say that they do not brainstorm very well together. Outside of these possibilities, you can refer to the development stages and behaviors below to gain an indication of your team's maturity level.

Forming

- Team members share information pertinent to the topic without being asked.
- Team members actively respond to questions when asked.

Storming

- Team members actively use brainstorming as a means to problem-solve.
- Team members engage in vigorous debate when needed and are able to separate issues from emotions.
- Team members are able to prioritize ideas and make a group decision.

Norming

- Team members suggest ideas for improving the team function.
- Team members create norms, rituals, and operating agreements.
- Team members actively follow the agreed-upon meeting rules.

Performing

- Team members actively acknowledge the contribution of other team members.
- Team members volunteer for task assignments.
- Team members communicate updates on tasks.
- Team members actively seek help when needed.

Transforming

- When team membership changes, the overall work of the team is able to continue without unreasonable interruption.
- Team members celebrate successes.

- Team members engage in "lessons learned" discussions without blaming.
- Team members ritualize the completion of major tasks or milestones.

These three assessment methods may not provide an exact scientific answer but act rather as indicators of development stage. Some teams may display characteristics of several stages. Do not let this confuse you into believing your team is a unique hybrid. You may simply have a team of high performers who have not learned to work together as a team. This is a short-term effect that will not manifest long-term success without some intervention by the team's leader.

Using Games to Develop Your Team

Once you have identified your team's stage of development, you are ready to select from a list of potential team-building games. When selecting a game, be aware of whether you are trying to reinforce the stage your team is currently in or you are challenging them to move to the next stage. Be careful not to push your team into the next stage too soon as you may cause unintended issues. The good news is that when you use a game that is beyond the development level of your team, you're going to find out quickly. Teams express a mismatch by just not participating or expressing feelings of "this is a waste of time." When you encounter these responses, you most likely have a mismatch. At this point, you should consider clarifying your purpose in doing the activity to ensure that everyone is on the same page. Sometimes by clarifying expectations you can reset people's feelings about the value of this activity. If you continue to get push-back to an activity, consider discontinuing that activity and shifting to an activity that addresses the needs of a team at a lower stage of development.

By matching the right game to the right stage of team development, you will assist in moving your team forward through the stages. These games are a great supplement to your ongoing team meetings. Think of them in terms of a resource you can pull out and use to continue to develop your team. You may find that utilizing a properly selected team-building game with your team can have a profound effect on team members' desire to work together more closely. As authors of this book, we are all practitioners of the games listed. We can say with no hesitation that the right game at the right time with the right people can have results beyond the expectations of the leader or team members. Don't be afraid to be different and give it a shot. That's what leadership is all about, right?

Using the Game Matrix

To make your selection of a game easier, use the following Game Matrix to quickly locate the game that will most meet your needs.

Game Matrix

√ Indicates the chapter (stage) where you will find the game

• Indicates other stages of group formation in which the game can be used

Games	Forming	Storming	Norming	Performing	Transforming
A Fresh Point of View				√	
A Graphic Description		√	•	•	
A Map of Our Team	√	•	•		
Advanced Virtual Q&A				√	
All About Me	√				
Alphabet Pyramid	√				
Around-the-Clock Recognition	•	•	•	•	√
Background Story	√				
Blind Origami		√			
BVTE			√		
Caricature Match Game	•	•	•	•	√

(continued)

Games	Forming	Storming	Norming	Performing	Transforming
Communication Best Practices		√	•		
Conference Call Bingo		•	√		
Count Off				√	
Digital Grapefruit	√				
DIY				√	
End on a High Note			√		
Entrance Music				√	
Escape from Wolf Island		√		•	
Five-Word Snapshot				√	
Flight 287 to Boston				√	
Grid Matchup		√	•	•	•
Haiku		√	•	•	•
Hear Ye		√	•	•	
I Hereby Recommend . . .					√
Intro 140	√				
Job Description			√		
Lessons Learned					√
Line Up		√			
Logic Puzzler		√	•	•	
Lunch Is on Me	•	•	•	√	•

Games	Forming	Storming	Norming	Performing	Transforming
Magic Wand		•		√	
Nickname Warp Speed	√	•	•	•	
Open Water		√			
Permission to Communicate	√				
Plus Deltas		√	•	•	
Project Spice Rack				√	
Rat-a-Tat-Tat		√			
Reality Check				√	
Same but Different			√	•	
Secret Coach			√	•	
Smashing Obstacles	•	√			
Speed PassPhrase		•		√	
Team ID	√				
Team Status Updates			√	•	•
Team Story			√		
Team Teach	•	•	√	•	•
Team Wordle: A Visual Picture of the Team	√	•	•		
Tell, Decide, Ignore			√		
Time Machine				√	
Ten for 10			√		
Tuned Out		√			

(continued)

Games	Forming	Storming	Norming	Performing	Transforming
Un-Virtually Yours		•	√	•	
Virtual Dessert			√		
Virtual High Fives		√		•	•
Virtual Q&A	•	•	√	•	•
Virtual Roundtable	√	•	•	•	•
Virtual Team Mascot	√	•			
Virtual Tic-Tac-Toe	√	•			
Walk the Plank				√	•
What's in a Name?	√				
Where Do You Stand?			√		
Who Are We?	√				
Word Cinquains					√
Yin and Yang				√	•

What Do I Need to Use These Games?

Tools and Technology

Most of the games and activities in this book can be played using technology and tools you already have. Internet access, email, and a good conference call service are the basic requirements for playing most of the games in this book.

In addition, many of the games in this book also require an online collaboration tool that allows team members to create, share, and edit documents together in real time. Your organization may already have tools available for your team's use. If not, a wide variety of web-based collaborative tools are available online.

Finally, additional tools and technologies can be used to help build your virtual work team. Social media sites, location-based map services, and even immersive "virtual world" technologies offer fun and engaging ways for team members to interact, build relationships, and create a strong sense of team spirit.

Choosing the Right Tools for Virtual Team Building

There are a number of things to consider when it comes to choosing a virtual collaboration tool that's right for your team. Your top priority is to choose one that allows for maximum engagement . . . that is, you'll want to choose a tool that's easy to use and implement, and that allows your team members to interact with few barriers.

Here are a few things you should consider:

- **Cost:** The economic conditions of recent years have led many organizations to look for cost-effective ways for teams to meet and interact. For most teams, virtual meetings are a great way to reduce the costs associated with traditional in-person meetings. Airfares, conference room fees, and many other travel expenses are eliminated when teams get together in the virtual world.

  A variety of technologies exist for virtual collaboration, ranging from free or low-cost web solutions to expensive customized software designed specifically for your organization. You'll find great tools at all ends of the cost spectrum. Many web-based tools offer a free version suitable for most small teams, along with paid versions that allow more users to collaborate and that include a set of enhanced features.
- **Ease of Use:** The ideal virtual collaboration tool has a user-friendly interface, with features that are easy to learn and understand. Prior to your meeting, team members should take the time to get familiar with whatever tool or technology you will be using.
- **An Engaging Interface:** One of the biggest challenges for teams that meet virtually is keeping members engaged. When you're not meeting face to face, it's tempting for team members to disengage from the process, whether to check emails, multitask on another project, or squeeze in one more game of Angry Birds.

  Choose tools that will keep everyone engaged and enjoying the experience. An attractive, easy-to-use interface will lead to a more satisfying virtual meeting than a cluttered and confusing interface.
- **A Proven Technology:** Look for technologies that have a proven track record or that are used by industry leaders. In today's climate of rapid innovation, new web-based tools are continually being created. Some become widely accepted while others are quickly forgotten. You'll want to choose a technology that will last, at least through the duration of your project.

- **Appropriateness for the Team:** It's important to choose a collaboration tool that matches the way your team members naturally prefer to communicate. Some team members like communicating by phone and conference calls, while others prefer email, texting, or instant messaging. It's a good idea to spend some time at the beginning of your project learning which modes of communication your team members like best.
- **Privacy and Security:** Keeping your organization's data secure should be a top consideration for virtual teams. Although none of the team-building activities in this book involve sharing critical company information, you should consult with your IT department to make sure your team is in compliance with company guidelines.

Tools and Technologies for Building Your Virtual Team

Building an effective virtual team can be challenging, but today's web-based tools make it easier than ever before. Here's an overview of some of the tools and technologies virtual teams can use to help build spirit, strengthen working relationships among members, and improve trust and communication.

Email, Texting, and Instant Messaging

Email continues to be one of the primary ways for virtual work teams to communicate. Because of its widespread usage, team members should understand some of the pros and cons of email.

Email is useful when a quick response is not necessary. It's also great for conveying basic information, but should be avoided if your message is complex or requires the input of several people. An email addressed to everyone on the team can quickly turn into a threaded message nightmare if it requires feedback and discussion from everyone.

An especially effective use of email is for virtual work teams whose members come from a variety of countries and whose native languages may be different from the rest of the team. These team members may have difficulty keeping up with a live conversation being spoken by native speakers. Email is especially useful in these cases.

The use of text messages and instant messages (IMs) has become more common in the workplace, especially among younger team members accustomed to communicating with friends and family via texting. Most text messages are limited to 160 characters. And although Shakespeare tells us that "brevity is the soul of wit," team members using text messaging should understand the limitations inherent in this brief form of communication.

Phone, Conference-Call, and Video-Conferencing Tools

Many people feel that a phone call or conference call beats an email or instant message for clear communication. The tone of a speaker's voice can convey things that might not be apparent in an email or text message. Phone conversations and conference calls let virtual team members share a good laugh together, understand the sense of urgency conveyed in a team leader's voice, appreciate the irony in a teammate's comment, or hang on every word of a colleague's well-told story.

It's likely that your organization is set up to host conference calls among team members. If not, there are a number of free and fee-based services you can choose from. The popular FreeConferenceCall (freeconferencecall.com) service is widely used by many organizations, ranging from small businesses to Fortune 500 companies.

GoToMeeting

What do I need to use these games? GoToMeeting

Fee-based web conferencing services like Cisco's WebEx (webex.com) and Citrix Online's GoToMeeting (gotomeeting.com) allow team members to easily meet and collaborate online. Both offer a user-friendly interface and a set of online collaboration tools including the ability for team members to share any screen or application on their computer with the rest of the group in real time. These services are great for many of the games and activities described in this book.

What do I need to use these games? Skype

Skype (skype.com) continues to grow in popularity, and now offers business-oriented collaborative tools like video conferencing, file and screen sharing, instant messaging, and more. Many of the virtual team-building activities in this book can be conducted using Skype's collaborative tools.

Online Collaboration and Document-Sharing Tools

A good online collaboration tool is a must-have for any virtual work team. Web-based collaborative tools allow team members to create and share documents, spreadsheets, drawings, and presentations with one another in real time. In addition to their potential for boosting a team's productivity, these tools provide a great platform for many of the team-building games and activities described in this book.

Virtual work teams can choose from a host of free and fee-based online collaborative tools offering a wide assortment of features to fit any budget. Some of today's most popular web-based collaborative tools, including Google Docs, Microsoft Office 365, Zoho, and Basecamp, offer an online experience perfectly suited for the virtual team-building games described in this book.

Google Docs (google.com/docs) is a free suite of online collaborative tools including word processing, spreadsheets, presentations, slide shows, and drawings.

Documents created with Google Docs are stored online on Google's servers, but can also be downloaded and saved to one's local computer in a variety of popular formats including Word, Excel, PowerPoint, PDF, and more. Similarly, documents created in these formats on one's local computer can be uploaded and saved to Google Docs in their original format, or converted to the Google Docs format.

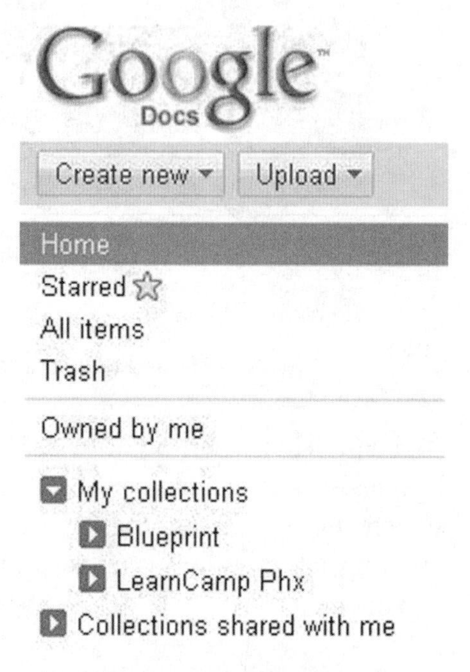

What do I need to use these games?
Google Docs

One of the strengths of Google Docs is its focus on real-time collaboration for users, making it great for virtual team-building games. Up to 50 team members at a time can work simultaneously on a shared document, and adding new team members is simple. Team members can edit a document, add comments, and chat with one another in real time. Google Docs keeps track of all changes made to a document so members can review every edit, reverting back to an earlier version if needed.

An expanded version of Google Docs is also available for users of Google Apps for Business, a fee-based service that provides a set of additional features, better security, and 24/7 technical support.

Microsoft Office 365 (office365.com) is a paid subscription-based service that includes a full set of Microsoft Office Web Apps. This service will feel familiar to users of Microsoft's well-established Office software suite. As one would expect, the cloud-based Office 365 is designed to be completely compatible with Microsoft Word, Excel, and PowerPoint. Like many other web-based collaborative tools, Office 365 is compatible with most mobile devices.

Office 365's emphasis on document sharing and online collaboration, combined with its tight integration with Microsoft's Office software suite, make it an attractive choice for virtual work teams and a solid platform for virtual team-building activities.

Zoho (zoho.com) and Basecamp (basecamphq.com) both offer a variety of online collaboration and productivity applications geared for business users. Each of these popular services gives users the ability to create and edit word-processing documents, spreadsheets, presentations, and more with fellow teammates simultaneously in real time. In addition, Zoho and Basecamp offer plug-ins that allow them to integrate with common office suites like Microsoft Outlook, Google Apps, and more. Both of these services are compatible with mobile devices including iPhones, Android phones, and BlackBerry devices, allowing virtual team members to collaborate on the go. Each is available in a variety of pricing options suitable for organizations of all sizes.

Location- and Map-Based Services

Location- and map-based services like Google Maps (google.com/maps), MapQuest (mapquest.com), Bing Maps (bing.com/maps), and Yahoo! Maps (maps.yahoo.com) provide a world of information for virtual work teams. These services allow team members to create and save customized maps identifying places of importance for the team, including the location of important clients and vendors, the location of the team's corporate and satellite offices, warehouses and distribution centers, and even the location of team members at any given time.

From a team-building perspective, map-based services give virtual team members an opportunity to collaborate on customized maps that allow them to get to know each other better and develop stronger working relationships. You'll find some fun map-based team-building activities in this book.

Social Networking Tools

Social networking sites and social media tools can play a key role in the development of a strong virtual team. By their very nature, social networking sites are designed to let users connect with friends and colleagues. However, not all social networking sites are appropriate for business use. Team members may share friendships that extend beyond the workplace, but may be cautious of using social networking tools that blur the lines between team members' work and personal lives.

Twitter (twitter.com) lets users instantly post short messages, or "tweets," of up to 140 characters from their computer, laptop, or mobile device. Commonly used by organizations as part of their marketing or public relations efforts, Twitter can also be a great tool for virtual work teams, provided they take steps to keep their tweets private.

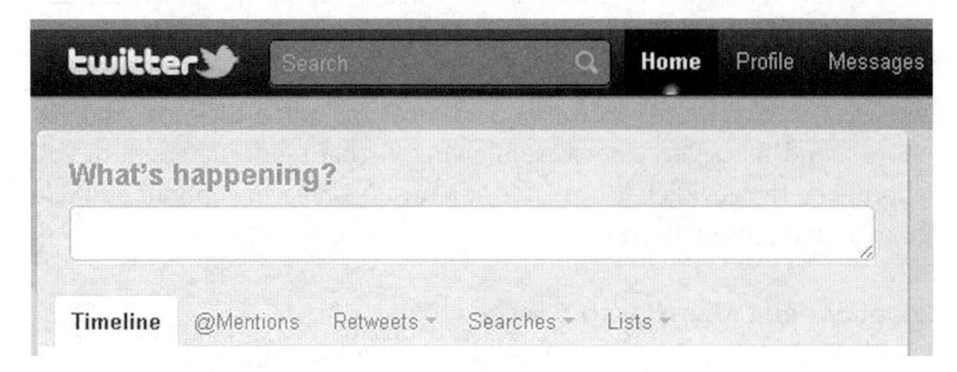

What do I need to use these games? Twitter

With Twitter, team members can post important project updates as they happen in real time, brainstorm or tweet a good idea to the rest of the team instantaneously, quickly share links to articles or websites, and help remote team members feel more connected. A number of team-building activities in this book can be conducted using Twitter.

If your virtual work team is thinking about using Twitter, take precautions to keep your team's tweets private. To prevent confidential information from showing up in Google's search results, team members should be sure to check the "Protect My Tweets" box when setting up their account. This will ensure that only people approved by the team member can view and follow his or her tweets.

A business-focused alternative to Twitter is Chatter (chatter.com), created by Salesforce (salesforce.com). By letting users set up private communication networks shared exclusively by members of their own company, Chatter gives virtual work teams an experience similar to Twitter, with the added comfort of knowing that all posts and updates from team members will remain private.

With over 100 million users, LinkedIn (linkedin.com) is the world's largest business-focused social networking site. LinkedIn lets registered users connect with colleagues, clients, and other trusted contacts around the world. With LinkedIn, users create an online profile that can include their work-related accomplishments, job history, educational background, professional affiliations, recommendations from colleagues, and more.

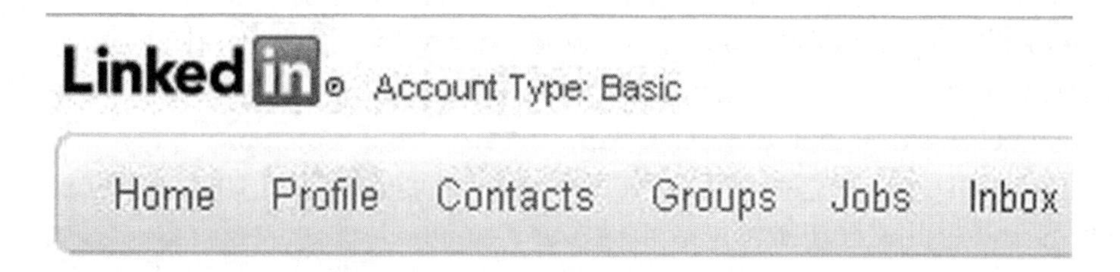

What do I need to use these games? LinkedIn

LinkedIn is a great way for members of newly formed virtual teams to learn more about fellow teammates and build connections with one another. It's a good practice at the start of a project to encourage everyone on the team to create a profile and add their fellow teammates to their list of trusted contacts.

As a virtual team completes a project or reaches an important milestone, team members can recognize one another's positive contributions to the team by posting a recommendation to their LinkedIn profile page.

A basic account with LinkedIn is free, with three paid upgrade levels available.

Facebook (facebook.com) is the world's most popular social networking site. Facebook has truly changed the way people interact, bringing together millions of people daily to connect with friends, family, colleagues, and classmates.

Although many colleagues and coworkers connect with each other on Facebook, virtual team members should keep in mind that some teammates may be uncomfortable mingling their work life with their personal life, and may therefore be reluctant to "friend" fellow teammates. Members of newly formed teams, where trust has not been fully established, should carefully consider that "friending" someone on Facebook allows that person to view any post, comment, or photo uploaded to your Wall . . . including posts that may be a little more personal than you wish to share with a new coworker.

Facebook is best for virtual work teams with a high level of trust, whose members have well-established friendships, or who have a long history of working together. Facebook is also great for virtual teams collaborating on a project of a public nature, such as a fund-raiser or charitable event.

Google+ (plus.google.com) is Google's entry into the world of social networking. Google+ has a number of features that make it an attractive social networking tool for virtual work teams.

Built with privacy in mind, Google+ allows users to sort their relationships and online connections into groups called Circles. Users can create as many Circles as they wish, including a Circle for members of their virtual team, a Circle for close friends or family, a Circle for acquaintances, or a Circle for just about any other group they belong to. Comments or updates posted to a Circle may only be seen by members of that Circle. A post shared with one's "virtual work team" Circle, for example, will remain private and visible only to members of that Circle.

A useful feature of Google+ is the video chat service called Hangouts. This service is well-suited for small virtual work teams, allowing up to ten people at a time to meet via live video stream. A member wishing to initiate a hangout for the team can specify that all members of that Circle are notified. Once connected, Google+ displays a live video stream of all the hangout members, focusing automatically on the person currenty speaking. Team members may also chat via Hangout's built-in group texting function.

Currently available by invitation from other Google+ users, this free service requires a Google account to get started.

Avatar-Based Virtual Worlds

Virtual worlds such as Second Life (secondlife.com) let team members meet and interact with each other in lifelike, fully immersive 3-D online environments. Users can visit these imaginary worlds by creating an avatar —a virtual figure or character to represent the user. In Second Life, avatars can explore destinations ranging from virtual versions of real places like Times Square or the Louvre in Paris to imaginative lands that may feel as if you've walked into a colorful impressionist painting or a fantasy movie set.

Work teams in Second Life can meet, brainstorm, and collaborate in contemporary-looking virtual conference centers that provide all the features one would expect in a real-life conference center. Team members can meet around a virtual boardroom table, write on a virtual whiteboard, display PowerPoint slides imported from real life and projected on a virtual screen, and hold small group discussions in private virtual breakout rooms.

A number of organizations offer team-building sessions designed especially for virtual work teams. These sessions tap into the fully immersive nature of Second Life to give virtual teams an experience that re-creates the team dynamics found in real-life team-building sessions.

Second Life is free, but users are required to download and install a special browser in order to explore it.

Getting the Most from This Book

Virtual teams are teams that are separated by distance, time, or both, and are connected by a shared purpose through the use of technology. The goal of the games in this book is to give members of your team a sense of togetherness even though they are physically separated. These games serve to build stronger relationships and help team members become more efficient while accomplishing their goals.

Many of these games provide a valuable lesson whether or not the participants succeed in the challenge. This is because the focus is on the process, the debriefing discussion, and how the experience can be applied to the workplace. As an added bonus, games allow team members to have fun while learning to work better together.

Selecting an Appropriate Virtual Team-Building Game

To make your selection of a game easier, use the Game Matrix on pages 19 to 22 to quickly locate the game that will best match the development stage of your team. In addition, each game description begins with:

- **Objectives**—the intended goals of the game
- **Team Size**—the recommended number of participants to properly run the game (for some of the games, it is recommended to split a larger team into smaller groups)
- **Materials**—any materials required to play the game
- **Time**—the total estimated time to complete this game
- **Technology**—the technology required to complete the game

These guidelines will help you determine the appropriate activity for your virtual team.

Stages of Group Formation

Virtual teams go through the same process as traditional teams: forming, storming, norming, performing, and transforming. While the virtual team experiences the same steps, those steps usually take much longer when working virtually. Some virtual teams never make it out of the storming stage because it's so easy to ignore conflict when you are separated by distance and time. The games in this book are sectioned into the particular stage of group formation that the game addresses. Check the Game Matrix on pages 19 to 22 to choose the right game for your team's stage in the formation process. Some games fit into more than one category. Some games can be played in an early stage of group formation and again at a later stage to gauge the changes the team has made over the course of the team members' time together.

You will notice more games for the first two stages, because time spent early on will more than pay off for your team in the long run. The games in the first two chapters focus on building trust, creating clear communication, and just getting to know the other people as people.

Ask members of your virtual team what is different about working on a traditional team from working on a virtual team, or what obstacles they have encountered with other virtual teams. Their answers will likely include the lack of everyday connections. The small talk, informal interactions, and nonverbal acknowledgments we enjoy when working in close proximity to other team members are usually nonexistent in virtual teams. The games in the first two chapters will help to overcome these common obstacles and increase the high-quality connections and likelihood of collaboration on the team.

Leading a Game

The team leader should facilitate the games in the first two stages of group formation because during these early stages the team looks to the leader to set the tone and provide direction. Games in the norming, performing, and transforming stages are opportunities for your team members to take on the role of leader/facilitator.

In a virtual team, there is a benefit in shared leadership. Working remotely, team members get used to being self-driven and in control of their world. Recognize and develop these leadership qualities by encouraging different team members to facilitate games. It's a great way to ensure everyone gets to shine in the leadership role.

Preparing Game Materials

For the virtual team-building games in this book, the materials are few. There is, however, prep time necessary for some of the games. Take into consideration the technology you would like the team to use and make sure it's up to the job. Most of the prep time is in emailing instructions or compiling and posting the results.

Get It Online at Our Website

Throughout this book, you will notice that you can "Get It Online." Go to virtualteambuildinggames.com for downloadable versions of many of the games. We have made it easy for you to get the necessary game materials to your team, no matter where they are located!

Introducing a Game

In general, give a brief explanation and background for the game. Provide a context for the activity to help team members to see how it contributes to your team's growth. Share appropriate information, such as any rules or guidelines, and answer any questions for clarification. Then assign the task, along with any time limits. Make sure to monitor the activity as it progresses, allowing enough time for the discussion questions.

Leading a Team Discussion

Most of the games include discussion questions to help the game leader facilitate a focused discussion after the activity. For some games, the team will generate discussion questions, and for a few games, no discussion is required. In addition to the discussion questions provided with the game's instructions, you may want to prepare other questions that are more tailored to suit your team or purpose. Let the team know the time allotted for the discussion. Keep your discussion concise and energetic to ensure a high level of engagement. Focus the team's attention on the meaning and purpose behind the game. Encourage the participants to be responsible for generating meaningful conversation; don't be too quick to insert your own opinions and observations.

Keep the discussion flowing, but also get comfortable with pauses as participants formulate their ideas and conclusions. End the discussion when all major points have been addressed. For virtual team discussions, it is a common practice for a team leader to draw the face of a clock and write everyone's name down at a different point on the clock. Then, as the discussion progresses, the leader can make sure everyone has had a chance to contribute and be heard by simply going around the clock.

High-Impact Debriefing

Discussing the experience is the key to realizing the relevance of the game and how it applies to your team. Without it, team members may not see the connection between what happened during the game and what happens "in real life." They may not understand the significance of their actions in the game until you discuss the debrief questions. To help the discussion flow smoothly, follow these guidelines:

- Take notes during the activity for reference during the debriefing discussion.
- Provide individuals with a copy of the questions before the full group discussion so they can note what they experienced during the game.
- Consider a "pair and share," especially in the first stages. After the game, have people pair up to discuss the questions, then bring the entire team together to recap the key points. This gives team members a chance to get to know each other better and is usually more comfortable for them until they get better acquainted.
- For large teams, have participants discuss the questions in small groups before the group discussion to ensure everyone gets a chance to contribute to the conversation.
- Get participants to discuss what happened in the game, what they learned, and how the learning applies in the workplace.
- Ask open-ended questions for a meaningful discussion.
- Ask—don't tell—participants about their experience, and how it relates to real-life situations.
- Use the discussion questions provided with each game as guidelines, not as a manual to be followed exactly.
- Adapt the ideas to what really happened in each game and what is really happening in the workplace.

Making the Transition to Real Life

All of the games in this book are broad in nature and not restricted to any single organization or industry. Your debriefing discussion, however, can be tailored to meet the specific needs of your team. When facilitating a game, it is important that you shift the team's attention from what happened in the activity to what is significant about the process that participants experienced as well as the results of their effort. Encourage participants to consider questions like "What will we remember from the game tomorrow?" "What can we take from this experience?" and "How can we use this experience to improve our team's communication?" You may consider making a record of the key learning points raised and action plans developed to post on your team's website or shared documents.

Tips for Using Virtual Team-Building Games

Here are some tips for getting the most out of virtual team-building games:

- **Have an objective.** High-performance teams want to be productive and use their time wisely, and some may perceive the game is taking the team away from important business. The games in the first chapter, which serve to create connections and develop trust, may seem frivolous at first glance. Remember that these games are serving to take the place of the informal connections and conversations that traditional teams experience in hallways and break rooms during the workday. These are the informal connections that have to be scheduled for a virtual team. Frontloading, or explaining the objective clearly at the beginning, will help the team understand the reason the game was chosen as well as the key issues and what to be aware of during the game. To ensure buy-in, after you explain the game, ask participants to provide their reasons the game is important, or how it can help build trust, improve communication, or increase the likelihood of success for the team.
- **Select the specific game carefully.** Look through the games to develop familiarity with the nature of each game, the objectives, and the materials, time, and technology required. Based on your objectives and where you believe your team is in their group development (forming, storming, norming, performing, or transforming), go to the corresponding chapter and choose a game to use with your team. Consider whether the particular game is a good fit for your team's general nature, the objectives for the team's meeting, and the participants themselves.
- **Have a backup plan.** It is especially important to have a backup plan at the beginning when all team members may not have the same skills regarding technology, or the technology itself may not be working

properly. Get creative and look for ways to be flexible with the way the game is played on your virtual team. If the team seems unresponsive, make sure technology is not the issue. Technological problems can create conflict within the team, and if that happens, remember to bring it up in your debriefing discussion. The games give the team a chance to test-drive technology and discover its challenges and benefits as well as what works and what doesn't.

- **Be brief and selective.** The majority of these games can be introduced and used in relatively short time periods. However, most games provide one or more discussion questions that will help you expand the conversation and derive greater value from the games. With a few exceptions, such as Communication Best Practices (page 95), the games themselves are not the focus of the experience. They are aids to achieve your goals and objectives. Don't drag the game out. Monitor the team's energy level and enthusiasm, and pace the activity accordingly.
- **Be creative.** Experiment a little. Search for ways to adapt or tailor a game to best fit your purpose for the team you're working with. Be on the lookout for new ways to make your point. Stay flexible.
- **Evaluate your use of games.** Keep track of: (1) the frequency with which you use games with your team; (2) the games' impact on your team's interpersonal relationships, communication, and level of trust; and (3) the team's reaction to and reception of team-building games.
- **Lighten up.** Take your task seriously, but don't take *yourself* too seriously. Team members will come to trust and believe in you when they see you as a real person—someone who can laugh at him- or herself and can be comfortable with minor deviations from the structured activity. Above all, have fun and make it fun for the team.
- **Be prepared.** After deciding to use a game, prepare for it thoroughly. Make certain that you are familiar with the game, you have downloaded the materials you need, your goals are clearly defined, and you have a specific plan for debriefing the group at the game's conclusion. Also be prepared to be flexible. Allow the team to go in an entirely different direction if that's what team members need from the game.
- **Anticipate recall of the game, not the message.** Because games are different from a classic work-oriented agenda, there is always a

chance that team members will remember the game or activity and forget the underlying message. Once the game is completed and you are ready to move on in your meeting, focus the team's attention once more on the key learning points. Chart the team's progress with the games on a team website.

Summary

The virtual team-building games in this book will help your team build trust, communicate more effectively, and overcome the inherent challenges of working virtually. You can meet many other objectives by using these activities. Games can be used to:

- Provide opportunities for informal interactions that traditional teams take for granted
- Help prevent the sense of isolation
- Build a stronger sense of team identity
- Encourage the use of different kinds of technology
- Increase skills in using diverse technology
- Examine process improvement
- Improve problem solving and decision making
- Uncover hidden problems
- Practice dealing with conflict
- Remind team members they are an important part of the team

The games help your team meet these goals in a fun way that makes team members feel more connected to each other as well as the team they have come together to create. Use these games to develop your "best virtual team ever."

1 Virtual Team-Building Games for the Forming Stage

None of us is as smart as all of us.

—*Japanese Proverb*

The Forming Stage

This is the polite, get acquainted, and "get to know each other" stage. This is where team members begin to figure out who's who, and where everyone fits into the picture. Typically, this takes place at the opening meeting or even an orientation session. For a virtual team, get a head start on this stage by providing the team with each team member's qualifications and background information so everyone has an understanding of why the individuals were chosen for the team.

For traditional teams, the forming stage includes both the actual time spent in meetings and the informal gatherings and discussions in and around the initial meetings. For virtual teams, these informal connections have to be planned for and strategically incorporated early on into team conference calls. The goal is to create an environment that is safe and secure. Because the team also looks for guidance and direction in this stage, the leader must ensure that the team's purpose is clearly communicated and understood by all team members. At this beginning stage, it's essential to get buy-in from all the team members and candidly and honestly identify the pros and cons of teamwork and team building. This stage is where the team builds their foundation, so time well spent in this stage will pay off later.

A Map of Our Team

OBJECTIVES

- To build a stronger sense of team identity
- To gain a better understanding of the members of the team

Team Size

Any

Materials

Landmark Suggestion List provided and available for download at virtualteambuildinggames.com

Time

20 minutes or more

Technology

Google Maps, Bing Maps, MapQuest, or other location- or map-based service. Everyone on the team will need an account to use any of these services.

Procedure

Online collaborative tools give virtual work teams a whole new set of resources for working together and building relationships among members. This activity uses an online location- or map-based service to create an interactive, customized (and private) map that's all about your team and its members.

Shared maps are a great way for team members to visualize where everyone lives and works, and provide opportunities for participants to learn more about their virtual teammates.

We suggest following these steps prior to the team meeting:

1. Assign a unique colored marker or pushpin to each team member.
2. Team members can place their pushpins anywhere on the map to identify landmarks that are related to them.
3. Team members can include as much or as little detail as they would like.

4. Once completed, people can click on the pushpins of their teammates to learn more about them, including fun facts, professionally relevant facts, information that's location-specific, and personal insights.

Landmarks should be as specific as possible and include work- or project-related places. Using the maximum zoom will ensure your pushpin locations are exact. Ideas for landmarks include:

- The place you currently work
- The location of your corporate headquarters
- The location(s) of key vendors, customers, or clients

Ideally, this game should focus on more personal aspects of team members' lives. In order for teammates to really get to know each other, make sure to include some nonwork categories for team members to mark on your shared map. Here are a few suggestions:

- Your hometown/where you grew up
- The college you attended
- A place you would like to live
- A place that intrigues you
- Sites of the three most significant experiences in your life
- A place you have visited several times
- The farthest place to which you have ever traveled
- The location of your favorite restaurant
- Where your child was born
- A favorite vacation spot
- All the places you have worked
- The location of your first job

Tips

An easy way to get started: navigate to maps.google.com.

- Click on "My places"
- Click on "Create new map"

Discussion Questions

1. How does sharing more personal information build a stronger virtual team?
2. Is self-disclosure necessary for a virtual work team? If so, what is the appropriate level of self-disclosure?
3. What are some other things we would like to learn about the members of our team?
4. How does geography play a role in a person's work style?

All About Me

OBJECTIVES

- To improve camaraderie and connections
- To understand more about the members of the team on a personal level
- To build a deeper level of trust on the team

Team Size

Any

Materials

All About Me Guidelines (provided here, and available for download from virtualteambuildinggames.com)

Time

10 to 20 minutes

Technology

Email, word-processing document

Procedure

While this activity is good for any type of virtual team, team members that are working from different time zones can gain a better sense of team by participating in this game. Request that each member of your team create an "All About Me" page (using the guidelines provided; add any other topics that may be of interest or unique to your team). Let them know the purpose of the task is to gain a better understanding of the people who make up the team. After receiving all the individual pages, combine them into one document and email it to all the team members to print out as a reminder of who the *people* are on their team.

Variations

After providing your team with the idea, ask them to submit topics of interest to be included in everyone's "All About Me" documents.

Discussion Questions

No discussion questions are necessary.

GET IT ONLINE!

All About Me Guidelines

Please create a document to help us to get to know you better. Start with your name and a current picture of yourself. Beneath your picture, complete these sentences.

- I was born in ________________.
- I live in ________________ and have lived here for ________________.
- My family consists of ________________.
- In my spare time I like to ________________.
- One of my favorite quotes is ________________.

Get creative! Pictures are welcome! Please include any additional pictures or interests that will help your teammates get to know you better. Thank you.

Sara Jensen

- I was born in Dodge City, Kansas.
- I live in Chicago, and have been here 12 years.
- My husband, Phil, and I have two sons. Zac is 7; Nick is 9. We have a dog, Sparky.
- In my spare time, I love to play soccer. I also love to read and am in a book club. (Do you have any book recommendations?)
- My favorite quote:
  "We are what we repeatedly do. Excellence then is not an act but a habit."
  –Aristotle

Alphabet Pyramid

OBJECTIVES

- To understand what it means to be a team member
- To discuss the challenges of maintaining a strong team when working virtually

Team Size

Any

Materials

Pen, paper, Alphabet Pyramids #1 and #2 and Scorecard (provided here, and available for download from virtualteambuildinggames.com)

Time

10 to 15 minutes

Technology

Online meeting software (with facilitator controlling the screen), conference call

Procedure

Split larger teams into smaller groups of four or five people, and if possible, have the same number of people in each group. Set up a separate conference call for each group. This game is played in two rounds. Each person will need a paper and pen.

A
BCD
EFGHI
JKLMNOP
QRSTUVWXYZ

Round One

Tell them you are going to show them a pyramid that contains all the letters of the alphabet. Let them know you will keep the pyramid on the screen for

A special thank you to Laurie Frank of GOAL Consulting (Goalconsulting.org) for this game.

10 seconds. While the pyramid is shown, their job is to memorize as many letters as possible. They may not write while the pyramid is on the screen.

Show Pyramid #1. After 10 seconds, blank out the screen and allow the team members to start writing down as many of the letters as they can remember—in the correct positions. When everyone is finished, reveal Pyramid #1 again so they can score their correct answers.

In their small groups, have them add up the number correct for each person and divide the total for the group by the number of people in the group to get an average individual score. Generally you will see scores between 6 and 10 (the number could be a decimal). Write their scores in the first column on the team scorecard.

Next, have each small group count how many they got correct as a group. If anyone in their group got a letter correct, they may count it, but each letter can be counted only one time. Scores usually range between 12 and 16. Fill in the scores in the second column on the team scorecard so everyone can see. This concludes round one.

Round Two

Tell the groups that you are going to show them another pyramid of letters, similar to the first, but the letters will be in a different order. This time, they are allowed to plan together how they want to memorize the letters as a team. Show them Pyramid #1 so they can plan. After two minutes of planning time, show them Pyramid #2 for 10 seconds. Blank out the screen and allow the groups to write the letters they memorized. When they are finished writing, put Pyramid #2 on the screen so they can score the correct letters, counting the number they got right as a group. Write these scores in the last column of your score sheet. You will usually see scores from 22 to 26.

For the discussion, put the discussion questions up on the screen and allow the small groups to discuss their experience for a few minutes before you open up the discussion to the whole team.

Tips

If your conference call service allows, set the telephone so that participants can all hear the facilitator and everyone in their small group. For the team discussion, open the phone line so everyone can hear and participate.

Discussion Questions

1. What is the difference between working as an individual, a group, and a team?
2. What makes a good team?
3. What are some challenges of a virtual team?
4. What can we do to overcome these challenges?
5. Please come up with three ideas our team can use to improve our virtual team.

GET IT ONLINE!

Alphabet Pyramids

Pyramid #1

Y

O N M

U X D A

C R L Z H

K J E G I P

S B Q T F V W

Pyramid #2

B

R Q P

X A G D

K U O J C

N M H F L S

V T E W I Y Z

Scorecard

Individual	Group	Team

Background Story

OBJECTIVES

- To get to know teammates better
- To build trust

Team Size
Up to 20

Materials
None

Time
10 to 15 minutes

Technology
Email, conference call

Once upon a time...

Procedure

Have team members email the game leader an interesting story from their past. The story can be work related or from one's personal life. The activity leader then copies all the stories into a single new email, taking care to remove any names or other details that may give away the storyteller's identity. Encourage team members to read each story prior to your next meeting. During your meeting, read one of the stories aloud and let the team guess or vote on whom the story belongs to. After team members submit their guesses, have the author of the story identify him- or herself. Do this for each of the stories. Stories can be varied in nature, as long as they are work appropriate.

Tips

You can theme your team's stories based on this list:

- Your first job
- Most interesting job you ever had

- Worst job you ever had
- Most interesting project you've ever worked on
- Most successful project you've ever worked on

Discussion Questions

1. What similarities do you notice in our backgrounds?
2. What were some of the most surprising background stories?
3. What background stories apply to our current project or work together?
4. Are there any lessons learned from our background stories that we can apply to our project or work together?

Digital Grapefruit

OBJECTIVES

- To explore new ways to communicate
- To encourage the use of different types of technology
- To become proficient with different types of technology

Team Size

Any

Materials

A picture of a recognizable object, such as a grapefruit

Time

Minimal time over the course of a few days

Technology

The more, the better. The goal of this activity is for team members to use as many different technologies as possible. This may include conference call, instant message, email, voicemail, fax, audio clip, or others.

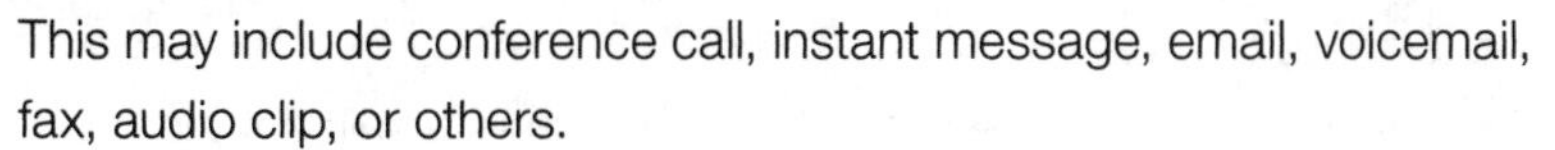

Procedure

This activity is a virtual version of the party game Pass the Grapefruit. Just as in the party game, team members are passing an item from person to person. In this version, however, the item has been specified by the game leader or facilitator and cannot be passed via the same method twice. This version also encourages friendly competition among and creativity in the members of your team.

1. The facilitator or game leader of this activity will select an object that is easily recognizable by everyone on the team.

2. The facilitator will split the team into two or more groups who will compete against each other. When possible, have the same number of participants in each group.
3. The leader will email everyone to let them know they are competing against the other groups to discover the greatest number of ways a concept can be electronically passed throughout the group.
4. Once a team member has used a particular technology, that same technology cannot be reused by someone else in the group. Let each team know it is up to them to track the technologies they have used. Remind them this is a competition and the team that uses the most technologies wins.

Here is an example:

- The facilitator sends a picture of a sailboat to team member one.
- Team member one emails a photo of a sailboat to team member two.
- Team member two faxes the photo to team member three.
- Team member three finds a video of a sailboat and sends a link to team member four via instant messaging.
- Team member four finds an audio clip of a sailboat on the ocean and calls team member five to share the link.
- Team member five opens a collaborative online tool and shares a sailboat picture with team member six.
- Team member six emails the facilitator each of the methods used to pass the object from each team member to the next.
- Once all groups have completed their task, the facilitator schedules a conference call to debrief the activity and allow team members to share their ideas.

Discussion Questions

1. Which technology was the first one to be used?
2. Which technology was the final one to be used?
3. Why was this one used last?
4. What was the most creative use of technology?
5. Did you work together as a team to identify the technologies you would use or was it up to each team member?
6. Were there any technologies used that you would like to understand better?
7. Were there any technologies that you avoided using? Why?

Intro 140

OBJECTIVES

- To practice active listening skills
- To describe or introduce another team member

Team Size

Any; team members work with partners

Materials

None

Time

15 to 20 minutes

Technology

Phone; team website or online collaborative tool, conference call for debrief discussion

Procedure

Intro 140 is a (very) brief way to introduce team members to each other, patterned after Twitter's "140-character-or-less" messages. Before your team meeting, assign each team member a partner and instruct him or her to call their partner for a one-on-one "get to know you" conversation prior to the next team meeting. At the conclusion of their conversation, each team member writes a 140-character introduction for their partner. In your team conference call, each person will introduce their partner by reading their 140-character message. Messages can also be posted on your online collaborative document or team website after the meeting ends.

Variations

Have team members create 140-character messages that describe the team or a team update.

Discussion Questions

1. How well did you listen to your partner?
2. How does "listening with purpose" affect the way we listen?
3. What does it take to listen effectively?
4. What can you do to improve your listening skills?

Nickname Warp Speed

OBJECTIVES
- To learn about teammates and build trust in a nonthreatening way
- To experience team problem solving and process improvement

Team Size
Up to 15

Materials
None

Time
20 to 30 minutes

Technology
Conference call

Procedure

This fast-paced problem-solving game starts with team members sharing a fun fact about themselves. Tell your team:

In the spirit of positive risk taking, please share with the team a nickname you like to be called, either from the past or the present. If there's a story behind the nickname, please share that too. I'll start, then we'll go around and hear from everyone. If you can't think of a nickname, you can invent one on the spot, or have the group help you come up with one.

After team members have shared their nicknames, say:

Now let's try to pass our nicknames around the group. We'll need to establish a communication pattern to do this. I will begin by saying my nickname, followed by the nickname of someone else in the group. When that person hears his or her nickname, that person will say the nickname, followed by the nickname of someone new. We'll continue the process until everyone in the group has spoken. The last person will say his or her nickname, followed by the nickname of the very first person who started the pattern.

Example:
Person 1 (Sneezy) says: Sneezy—Wiggles!
Person 2 (Wiggles) says: Wiggles—Motor Mouth!
Person 3 (Motor Mouth) says: Motor Mouth, and so on.

Once the team has established the pattern, have them repeat it once or twice to make sure they have it memorized.

Finally, challenge the team to achieve Nickname Warp Speed by setting a time goal for saying their nickname pattern. The rules are:

1. The team should set a time goal that's challenging, yet doable.
2. The team gets three attempts to reach their time goal.
3. Team members may take a few minutes for brainstorming between each attempt.
4. A one-second penalty will be added to the team's time whenever someone speaks out of sequence or otherwise messes up.
5. If the team hits their goal, they can use any remaining attempts to try for an even faster score.

Discussion Questions

1. Were you comfortable sharing your nickname with the team? Why or why not?
2. Is self-disclosure necessary for a virtual work team? If so, what is the appropriate level of self-disclosure?
3. What strategy did your team use to achieve Nickname Warp Speed? Was the strategy clear to everyone?
4. How did the team react if someone messed up?
5. In real life, what are some constructive ways of dealing with mistakes?

Permission to Communicate

OBJECTIVES

- To gain a better understanding of other team members' preferred communication styles
- To deepen trust on the team

Team Size

Any

Materials

Team Communication Matrix (provided here, and available for download from virtualteambuildinggames.com)

Time

5 to 10 minutes

Technology

Online collaborative tool, conference call for debriefing discussion

Procedure

Share the Team Communication Matrix with all team members using an online collaborative tool. Have each person fill out his or her own row of the matrix. Review the online document and lead the debriefing discussion at the next team meeting. Team members can refer to the completed Team Communication Matrix when communicating with one another, so be sure to post it in a prominent place such as the team website or distribute the completed matrix to all team members.

Discussion Questions

1. How does it benefit the team to better understand the communication preferences of the individuals on the team?
2. In addition to respecting each other's preferences, what can we do to create better communication on the team?
3. When does communication start to break down?
4. What can each of you do to be better communicators?

GET IT ONLINE!

Team Communication Matrix

Please answer these communication questions in the corresponding cells of the matrix.

Name: Type your name

Preferred: What is your preferred communication mode? Email? IM? Phone? Text?

911: If an immediate reply is needed, what is the best way to reach you?

Feedback: How do you like to receive feedback?

Conflict: How do you prefer to deal with conflict?

Recognition: How do you like to be complimented or what do you consider to be a compliment?

Name	Preferred	911	Feedback	Conflict	Recognition

Team ID

OBJECTIVES

- To create a team identity
- To make tangible the concept of "team"

Team Size

Up to 20

Time

20 to 30 minutes

Technology

Email, conference call

Procedure

The team members are tasked with creating a team identity so team members feel more connected to one another, resulting in more meaningful work conversations and a deeper level of trust.

1. For larger teams, create smaller brainstorming groups of four to seven people. This allows people to begin to form trusting relationships in a more comfortable small group rather than being overwhelmed by a large team.
2. Email all team members the brainstorming group assignments along with your request that they connect with their small group and think about the larger team they have come together to create. Remember this is the whole team they are considering, not just the four to seven members of their brainstorming group.
3. To help start their discussion, include in your email some brainstorming questions. Ask that they take a few minutes before the Team ID conference call to answer:
   - How would you describe our team?
   - What is our team personality?
   - What do we do well?
   - Who are we?

- How do our customers see us? How do our peers see us?
- What's great about our team?

4. When you bring your whole team together, ask a representative from each brainstorming group to share the group's answers to the questions. Starting with the first question, invite group representatives to share their responses, so that the information is organized.
5. Once you hear from everyone, it's time for the team to put it all together to create the Team ID. Ask the team to create:
   - A team name
   - A team logo
   - A team mascot
   - A team slogan
6. Have the team members use the team name and motto as part of their signature line when emailing one another.

Variations

After the team has decided on their Team ID, hold a contest to see who has the most team spirit. Give team members two days to decorate their workspace based on the team identity. Have each person take a picture of his or her workspace and submit it for judging. Give out fun awards such as "Most Colorful," "Best Use of the Space," or "Most Impressive Rendition of the Mascot," or simply a single award for "Best Team Spirit."

Discussion Questions

No discussion questions are necessary.

Team Wordle: A Visual Picture of the Team

OBJECTIVES

- To paint a visual picture of the virtual team
- To discover what team members have in common
- To understand the qualities that make this team unique

Team Size
Any

Materials
None

Time
10 minutes

Technology
Email; Wordle, a free Web-based tool for generating "word clouds," available from wordle.net; conference call for debriefing discussion

Procedure

This game provides a colorful, visual portrait of your team to print and share. Using the fun web-based tool Wordle, you will create an image that highlights the qualities your team members have in common as well as those that make your team unique.

Have each team member email a short written bio (100 words or less) to the facilitator. The facilitator will combine all of these bios together into one text file. This combined text will then be used to create a "Wordle," a visual depiction of the individual words used in the various team member bios.

In this team Wordle, the words that show up most frequently in the team's combined bio will appear large, while the less-common words will appear small. Play with the color, direction, and font settings to get the effect you want. Save your Wordle as a PDF and send it to everyone on the team. The facilitator can paste the Wordle image into a slide and share it with the team during an online meeting to guide the debriefing discussion. Encourage team members to print the Wordle as a reminder of the shared and unique characteristics that different team members bring to the project.

Discussion Questions

1. What are the topics we have most in common as a team?
2. What are the topics we have least in common as a team?
3. What are some trends you see from this picture?
4. What do you find most interesting about this Wordle in regard to the work we need to do as a team?

Virtual Roundtable

OBJECTIVES

- To have a visual to go along with your conference call meetings
- To remind your team who is on the call and who is part of the team

Team Size

Any

Materials

Profile photos of all team members, Virtual Roundtable template (available for download from virtualteambuildinggames.com)

Time

10 to 15 minutes of prep time

Technology

Online collaborative tool

Procedure

Virtual Roundtable is a creative way for team member to *see* each other during conference calls. Download the Virtual Roundtable template where you can drop in profile photos of all the team members attending your virtual meeting. You can also add team members' names, geographic location, title, or any other helpful information to the table. Encourage team members to keep the Virtual Roundtable displayed on their computer screens for the duration of your meeting.

Tips

The time needed for this activity is all prep time. Delegate a different team member each meeting to find out what team members will be in attendance and to create the virtual roundtable for the meeting.

Discussion Questions

1. What is the benefit of "seeing" each other during our meetings?
2. What are some ways we can remind ourselves that we are part of a team when working remotely?

Virtual Team Mascot

OBJECTIVES

- To create a team mascot representing the traits of an ideal team member
- To have some fun together while identifying shared team values

Team Size

Any

Materials

None

Time

25 minutes

Technology

Conference call, online collaborative tool that includes a drawing feature

Procedure

Spend 5 to 10 minutes brainstorming with your team to generate a list of personality traits and skills that an ideal team member would possess. Use the online collaborative tool to track ideas. Your list should contain items that would be common for any team, as well as traits unique to your specific team. Encourage team members to go beyond the obvious.

After brainstorming, use the drawing feature of your online collaborative tool to create a team mascot representing your ideal team member. It's fun to create your team mascot together in real time, with all team members contributing something to the drawing.

Your team mascot can be as simple as a stick figure or as elaborate as your team members' creativity allows. Be sure your team mascot depicts the traits your team identified in the brainstorming list. For example, if listening is one of your important traits, give your team mascot a pair of oversize ears.

Here are some suggestions for creating a great team mascot:

- Use a variety of colors, brushes, and shapes.
- Encourage each team member to add something to the drawing.
- Include clarifying words or labels to the drawing if you wish.

Have fun with this activity. Be sure to give your team mascot a name, and keep it posted on your team's website.

Variations

Teams that can't work together in real time can create their team mascot over the course of a few days. Each team member should contribute to the drawing when his or her schedule allows.

Discussion Questions

1. How was this activity useful for our team?
2. What are the most important traits needed to be a member of our team?

Virtual Tic-Tac-Toe

OBJECTIVES

- To improve virtual meeting skills

Team Size

Up to 8

Materials

Tic-Tac-Toe board (available for download from teambuildinggames.com)

Time

5 to 10 minutes

Technology

- Online collaborative tool or online meeting software, phone or VoIP

Procedure

Use this activity during an online meeting to reinforce positive solutions to dealing with the challenges of working together virtually. Break the group into two teams, Xs and Os. Explain to the team that in this game the Xs signify an issue or challenge for the team, and the Os signify a positive solution for the issue.

Each team takes turns placing a mark on the Tic-Tac-Toe board in hopes of winning. Team X starts by placing an X on the board along with a short explanation of a situation or issue that is challenging the team. The Os try to block the Xs by making a suggestion of a positive way to deal with that issue.

This continues until one team wins or loses. After the team finishes a game, have them switch roles. The Os are now Xs; the Xs are now Os. Play a minimum of two games so everyone has a chance to consider both views.

Example game: Team X suggests the issue "neglecting to mute your phone line when in a loud place" and places their X on the board (or the facilitator can place an X in the space on the board corresponding to their request). Team O suggests the solution "ask everyone to use mute when not speaking at the beginning of the call" to block the challenging issue and states where they want their O to be placed. This continues until one team wins or there is a tie. The game is cleared and you may start again.

After playing at least two rounds, the facilitator can begin the debriefing discussion.

Tips

Have each team appoint a scribe to track the problems and solutions. These ideas can be summarized and emailed to the team or posted on the team website or shared database for reference.

Variations

This game can be used in any stage of group development. The team can use the Xs and Os to signify any current challenges they are experiencing and possible solutions to those challenges.

Discussion Questions

1. Which challenge that was suggested is the one we experience most frequently?
2. Does the suggested method of dealing with it really work? If not, how could we do it better?
3. Which challenge is the hardest to deal with or find a solution to? Why?

What's in a Name?

OBJECTIVES

- To get to know the team members on a more personal level
- To build respect and understanding for others on the team
- To develop trust

Team Size
Up to 20

Materials
None

Time
10 to 30 minutes

Technology
Email, conference call

Procedure

Play this game early in your team's formation stage. Send an email to members of your team, letting them know that you will start your next team meeting with a game to help them get to know each other better. Tell them that each person will have the floor for a few minutes to tell the team the story of his or her name: such as what it means, where it came from, and perhaps the reason your parents had for giving you the name (this may require some prep time for team members). Ask them to close with, "I prefer to be called . . ."

Especially with a globally dispersed team, you can learn quite a bit about someone else with this low-risk, easy game. This can be a rich activity for a diverse team. In fact, the greater the diversity in the team, the more meaningful this activity is.

Thanks to Jim Cain, Ph.D., of Teamwork and Teamplay (teamworkandteamplay.com) for this activity.

Tips

By sending out the email beforehand, you will ensure that team members are ready with their story.

Variations

This activity can also be used to reveal the story behind other names such as participants' nicknames, pets' names, or children's names.

Discussion Questions

1. How important are names?
2. In what ways does the story behind our names define us?
3. Why is it important to remember and to use names?
4. How does this relate to trust within the team?
5. What are some ways to remember names and make sure we are pronouncing them correctly?

Who Are We?

OBJECTIVES

- To quickly learn more about team members in a way that goes beyond the obvious
- To encourage camaraderie and connections among team members

Team Size

Up to 12

Materials

One or both of the Who Are We? graphics (provided and available for download from virtualteambuildinggames.com)

Time

15 minutes

Technology

Conference call, online collaborative tool

Procedure

This is a simple, fun game to do with new teams who will be working together for an extended time. If your team is already established or your team project will be short in duration, this may not be the best choice for your team. This game gives people an opportunity to get to know teammates beyond work experience or job title. Keep the discussion fun and interactive and allow time for everyone to share. Who Are We? is an activity that brings about lots of discussion and sharing.

Using your online collaborative tool, display one of the Who Are We? graphics. Each graphic contains eight smaller images (labeled A through H for easy reference). Select one of the small images and ask if there is anyone on the team who has personal experience regarding the selected image. Have them share their experience with the team. The facilitator can ask the following questions to help guide the discussion.

Questions for Who Are We? 1

A. Who enjoys cooking, baking, or preparing special meals?
B. Who enjoys working with their hands mechanically: car repair, carpentry, working around the house?
C. Who enjoys teaching, public speaking, or facilitating groups?
D. Who enjoys extreme outdoor sports like rock climbing, snowboarding, mountaineering, or mountain biking?
E. What women in our group are mothers, stepmothers, grandmothers, aunts, cousins, or friends who play an important role in the lives of children?
F. What men in our group are fathers, stepfathers, grandfathers, uncles, cousins, or friends who play an important role in the lives of children?
G. Who are our book lovers? Do you read books electronically? Do you read blogs online?
H. Who enjoys water-based activities like sailing, rowing, or swimming?

Questions for Who Are We? 2

A. Who are our bowlers? Are there any bowlers who regularly bowl in the 200s?
B. Who loves spending time outdoors fishing?
C. Who are our sports nuts? Do you play sports or are you a big fan of sports? What is your favorite sport? What team are you passionate about? Do you have season tickets?
D. Who are our technology folks? Do you use social networking to connect with people?
E. Who are our class clowns? Did you get in trouble when you were a kid for being funny in class?
F. Who are our world travelers? What are some of the countries or states you have visited?
G. Who loves spending time in the mountains for rest and relaxation?
H. Who loves spending time on the beach for rest and relaxation?

Tips

Consider selecting a few of these images rather than trying to get through them all in one sitting. You may find it convenient to choose a few images to talk about at the beginning of each of your first few meetings to encourage ongoing team member sharing.

Variations

Have each team member bring a photo or image that represents an activity that he or she loves. Give each person an opportunity to share his or her photo and invite team members who share that interest to tell their story as well. Encourage team members to share stories rather than just facts. Sharing stories in an open and nonthreatening way will help move your team into later stages of development.

Who Are We? 1

Who Are We? 2

Discussion Questions

1. What was most surprising about the background of our team?
2. Why is it useful to understand more about the people you will be working with?
3. Did you find something unique that you have in common with another team member?

2

Virtual Team-Building Games for the Storming Stage

When we are debating an issue, loyalty means giving me your honest opinion, whether you think I'll like it or not. Disagreement, at this stage, stimulates me. But once a decision has been made, the debate ends. From that point on, loyalty means executing the decision as if it were your own.

—*Colin Powell*

The Storming Stage

In this stage, interpersonal issues may arise. This stage is typically where conflict gets introduced into a previously safe and comfortable environment. These conflicts provide team members with opportunities to learn how to interact effectively with one another. For a traditional team, this stage takes place around week two, when things that may not have mattered in the beginning suddenly seem important; therefore conflict ensues. You may experience this stage closer to week three or four, or even later, in a virtual team. This will depend on the frequency of communication on the team, and how much trust and camaraderie was developed in the forming stage.

This stage can be extremely frustrating when working virtually. Or it can be ignored completely. Out of sight, out of mind, so to speak. Some virtual teams never make it out of this challenging stage. While face-to-face communication allows for immediate feedback and provides nonverbal clues for better understanding, your virtual team may struggle with this stage, and become frustrated with the time it takes to resolve conflict and learn the best ways to communicate with other team members. The team will look to the leader to support them as they navigate through this stormy stage.

Many issues can cause separation on a team. Virtual teams are teams that are already separated—by distance, time, or both. To ensure that other issues don't arise to fracture your team, develop protocols for using various types of technology, along with training to ensure that all team members are comfortable and willing to use the best technology for the situation. The one-way nature of email, which is one of the main communication methods teams use, hinders a team's ability to navigate through conflict. Use the games in this section to give the team a chance to practice conflict resolution and also to open the door to a team discussion about conflict. It is critical that these concerns be dealt with honestly. When interpersonal conflicts and dissonance are handled at this early stage, the team has a better chance of success. Once again, leadership will be necessary to navigate through this stage, so the team leader should facilitate the games in this section. The leader should also lead discussions to ensure the team can use these tools when interacting with each other day to day.

A Graphic Description

OBJECTIVES

- To understand the limitations of one-way communication such as email
- To improve verbal communication skills

Team Size
Any

Materials
Graphic Description illustration (provided here, and available for download from virtual teambuildinggames.com), paper and pen

Time
10 to 15 minutes

Technology
Phone; email; optional: online collaborative tool or team website

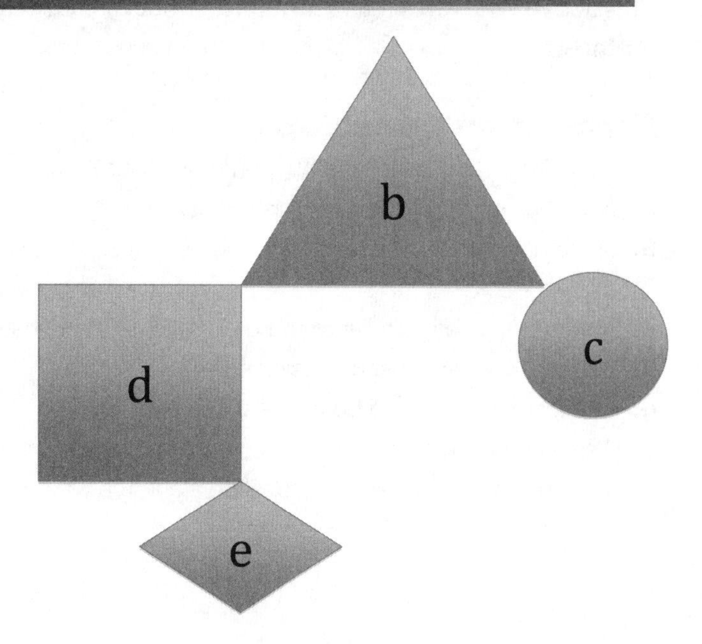

Procedure

One team member will describe an image to the rest of the team without the benefit of two-way communication.

1. Send the image to one team member, either by scanning the page at the end of this game or by emailing the electronic version from the book website.
2. Have all other participants get a paper and pen.
3. The team member with the drawing has to describe the picture to the rest of the team while they draw exactly what is communicated. Team members can ask no questions (this is to simulate the one-way nature of email communication).

4. When finished, the facilitator either displays the original image on the screen or emails it to the team. If you have company intranet, it's fun to post the original there and ask your team to post their versions so everyone can see each other's interpretation of the instructions. Be sure to thank the communicator for taking on a challenging task.

Tips

This activity can provide meaningful input to your team's communication protocols.

Discussion Questions

1. Team, how successful was our communication?
2. What was challenging about this activity?
3. Communicator, what was it like to give directions without getting any feedback?
4. How is this activity similar to using email to communicate?
5. What are your experiences using email?
6. As a team, what would be the best use of email?
7. What can we do to improve our communication with each other?
8. If you could have asked one question along the way, what would it have been?

GET IT ONLINE!

A Graphic Description

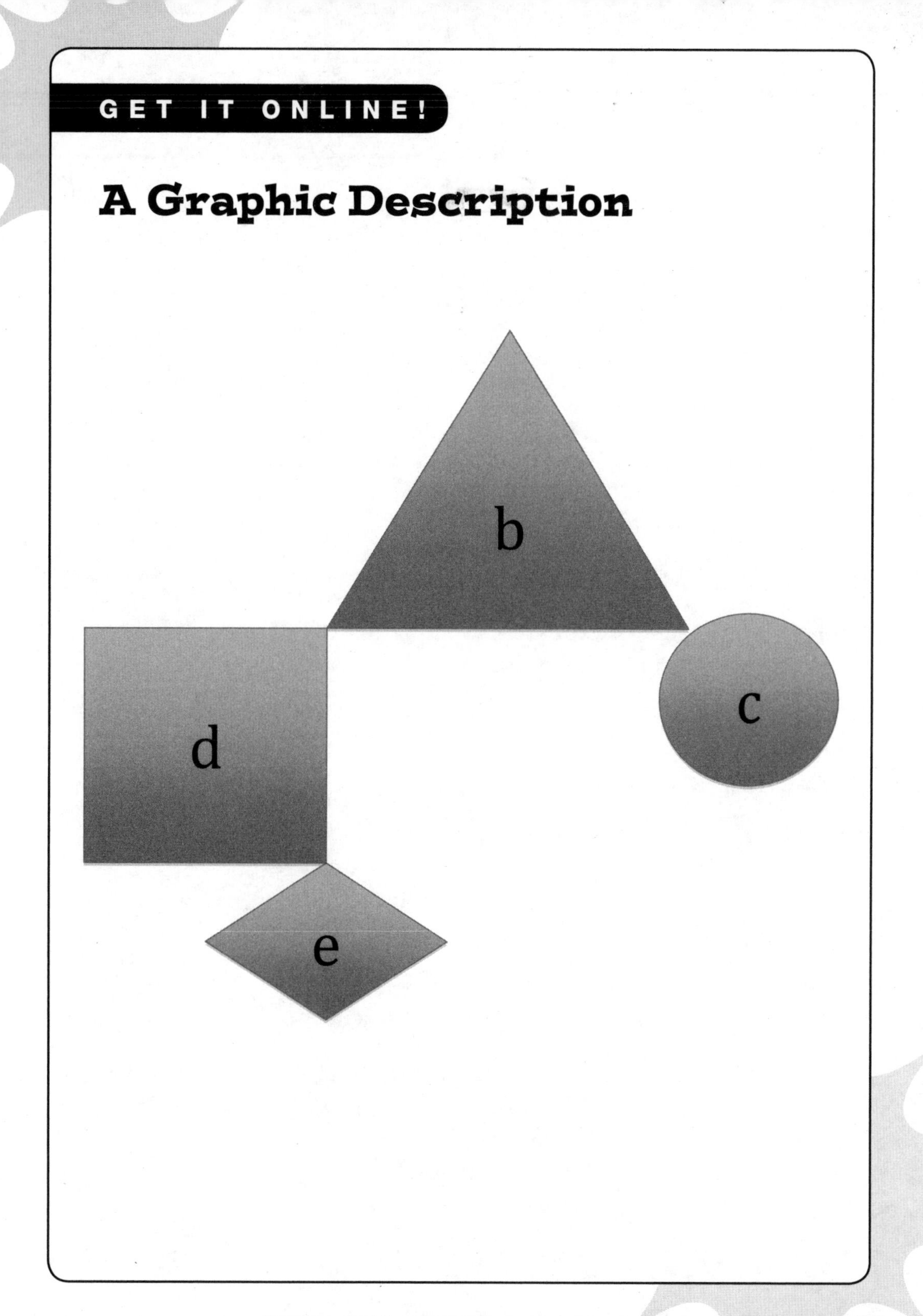

Blind Origami

OBJECTIVES
- To build verbal communication skills
- To highlight the importance of listening and asking for feedback

Team Size
Any; team members work with partners

Materials
Two different sets of simple illustrated origami instructions (one set for each person in the pair); many websites provide simple origami instructions; we recommend Origami-Fun (origami-fun.com) for its easy-to-follow illustrations and its free, downloadable PDF files; one 8½ x 11 sheet of paper per person

Time
25 to 30 minutes

Technology
Email, phone

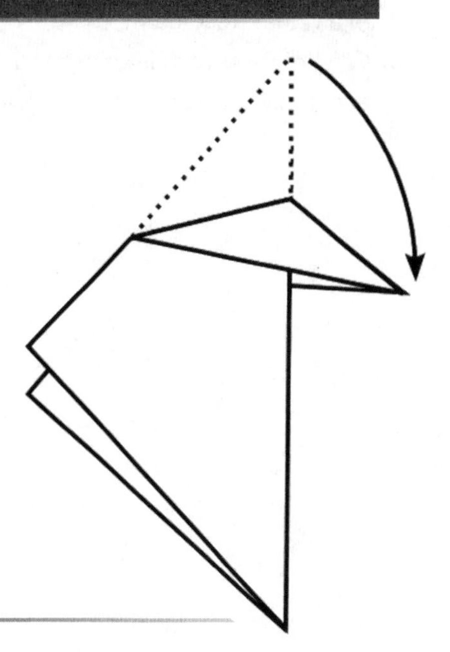

Procedure

Assign or have team members form partnerships. Email each partner a different set of illustrated origami instructions.

Using verbal communication only, one team member attempts to guide his or her partner through the steps required to create a folded origami sculpture out of the 8½ × 11 sheet of paper. The partner receiving the instructions may ask questions, request clarification, and offer feedback at any point during the process. When finished, each team member who gave the instructions will email the original instructions to his or her partner to compare the final product to the original instructions.

Have the partners switch roles and repeat the process, using the different set of illustrated origami instructions.

Discussion Questions

1. Which role did you find most challenging: communicator or listener? Why?
2. What were some things your guide did that were helpful for you as a listener?
3. Are there things you or your partner could have done differently that would have improved your level of success?
4. What are some of the communication challenges you face in real life as part of a virtual work team?
5. What did you learn from this activity that can help you communicate more effectively with your virtual work team?

Communication Best Practices

OBJECTIVES

- To create team communication norms
- To demonstrate effective communication practices

Team Size

Any

Materials

Communication Best Practices Worksheet (provided here, and available for download from virtualteambuildinggames.com)

Time

1 hour or more

Technology

Email, conference call, online collaborative tool, team web book or website

Procedure

For virtual teams, creating norms is essential. Norms can help teams create consistency, lessen conflict, and promote accountability, and can help team members feel more connected to each other and the team.

Once created, post your team norms in a team Web book or online resource that the team can access at any time. This activity focuses on communication norms, but you can follow this process to create other team norms, rituals, and operating agreements. Once the team decides on the norms they will adhere to, writing them in a positive manner is important. For example, have them come up with "what to do" rather than "what not to do." Posting team norms in a prominent place like your team website or web book increases their value.

Follow these steps to generate your team's best practices regarding communication:

1. Email the worksheet to team members to be completed before your next team meeting. Have them complete the form on their own without discussing their answers with other teammates.
2. Ask the team members to list all the qualities and characteristics of good communication practices. Request that they provide examples for each item and be prepared to provide the reasons they included this item on their list. Allow 20 minutes for this step.
3. During the next team meeting, have team members share the items on their list. During this stage of the activity, other team members are to listen, ask questions for clarification, and provide positive feedback. Suggest they use the technique of listening "for" rather than "against" the speaker. Their job is not to judge the items on another team member's list, but to gain clarity and understanding.
4. The team comes together using the online collaborative tool to create their Team Communication Best Practices. If your team is larger than ten members, you may want to do this part as a two-step process, where small groups of five or six team members collaborate on their group list, after which they take it to the entire team. Drawing from all the ideas detailed on the individual lists, the team needs to collaborate to create team norms regarding the positive communication practices that team members will follow during their time together.
5. Post the completed list on your team website or include it in your team's web book. Refer to the list during future meetings or as part of the debriefing discussion in a communication game such as Speed PassPhrase (page 211).

Use this list as a living document, and revise the list as needed to reflect the team's changing needs and dynamics during the duration of your virtual team.

Tips

Use this activity in conjunction with Line Up (page 113). Line Up should be played in one meeting, and this activity should be run in the meeting that immediately follows. During your Line Up debriefing discussion, be sure to talk about the benefits of developing team norms for communication. At the end of the discussion, let them know you will email a form to be completed before the next team meeting. This will set the stage to jump right into Step #3 of this activity.

In developing their lists, the team will put to use many of the components of effective communication, making this an activity within an activity!

Variations

Some virtual teams have the opportunity to meet in person at the beginning of their project. If this is the case for your team, include this activity as part of the initial face-to-face meeting. After facilitating some icebreakers and climate-setting games, move on to this activity. Once completed, use the Team Communication Best Practices to help create your team's goals, vision, and mission statement.

Discussion Questions

1. What was the hardest part of creating our team communication norms?
2. What are the benefits of shared norms?
3. How can we hold each other accountable for following the agreed-upon norms?
4. Can we do this in a positive manner?
5. What would that look/sound like?

GET IT ONLINE!

Communication Best Practices Worksheet

List the qualities/characteristics of the best communication practices. For each item listed, please provide an example and the reason the item is on your list.

1. ______________________________

Example:

____

____

____

____

The reason this quality/characteristic is on my list: ______________________________

____

____

____

____

2. ______________________________

Example:

____

____

____

____

GET IT ONLINE!

The reason this quality/characteristic is on my list: ______________________

____

____

____

3. ____

Example:

____

____

____

____

The reason this quality/characteristic is on my list: ______________________

____

____

____

____

4. ____

Example:

____

____

____

____

GET IT ONLINE!

The reason this quality/characteristic is on my list: ______________________

____

____

5. ____

Example:

____

____

____

The reason this quality/characteristic is on my list: ______________________

____

____

____

6. ____

Example:

____

____

____

The reason this quality/characteristic is on my list: ______________________

____

____

____

Escape from Wolf Island

OBJECTIVES

- To develop team problem-solving skills
- To enhance team communication

Team Size

Up to 12

Materials

Picture of an island in the middle of a lake (available for download from virtualteambuildinggames.com); Escape from Wolf Island List of Resources (provided here, and available for download from virtualteam buildinggames.com)

Time

20 minutes

Technology

Conference call, online collaborative tool

Procedure

The game leader begins the activity by displaying the picture of the island in the lake. Tell the team there are four people stranded on the island. Explain that this group was separated from their larger group while on a hike to a nearby island waterfall. The rest of their group took a boat across the lake back to the mainland. This stranded group must get off the island and back to the other lake shore before darkness falls, as they are not prepared to spend the night on this remote island. Using resources found on the island (see list provided), the team must plan their escape.

Also important to note, only two of the team members can swim. The distance to shore is too far for one person to swim the entire way. Either of the two swimmers could make it three-quarters of the way before getting too exhausted. The stranded team has just less than two hours before nightfall, which is just long enough to swim across the lake to shore once. Last, the island has wolves, so no one can be left behind . . . if you get my drift!

The resources have some rules governing their usage, which must be followed. The game leader should prepare a slide with the provided list of resources.

The purpose of this game is to brainstorm possible solutions. There is no single answer to this puzzle. Encourage your team to be creative and consider several potential solutions. In the end, your purpose is to engage team members' critical thinking and team problem solving.

Discussion Questions

1. What was the most important item that someone brought?
2. What proved to be the most effective skill in coming up with workable solutions?
3. Do you feel everyone's voice was heard in coming up with potential solutions?
    a. If yes, what did the team do to encourage everyone's input?
    b. If no, what could have been done to increase the level of input?
4. How does this activity mirror our own team and our process of problem solving?

GET IT ONLINE!

Escape from Wolf Mountain List of Resources

- Chain—the chain cannot be cut as there is nothing strong enough to cut it
- Ball of twine—30 feet long
- Gopher—just a brown gopher chilling out on the shore
- One wooden oar
- Children's inner tube—can support the weight of one adult
- Two 3-foot logs—does wood float?
- A beer bottle—with no cap
- Duct tape—the only tool you really need
- Hamster wheel—where the heck did this come from?
- Four Ping-Pong paddles
- Bicycle chain
- Partially deflated beach ball
- Large beach towel

Grid Matchup

OBJECTIVES

- To collaborate and achieve consensus as a team
- To experience team problem solving

Team Size

4 to 9

Materials

The nine Grid Matchup photo pieces (labeled A through I), along with the Master Photo showing the completed solution (available for download from virtualteambuildinggames.com)

Time

25 to 30 minutes

Technology

Email, conference call

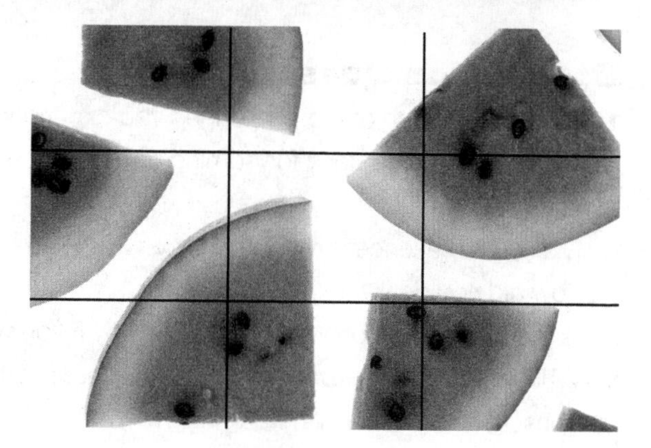

Procedure

1. Distribute via email all nine of the Grid Matchup photo pieces to your team members. If you have fewer than nine people, give some people two pieces. Do not distribute the Master Photo; keep it for yourself.
2. Inform your team members that the nine Grid Matchup photo pieces are all parts of one large Master Photo. The Master Photo has been chopped into nine pieces like a three-by-three Tic-Tac-Toe grid.
3. Using verbal communication only, the team must discuss and decide where each of the nine pieces fits into the three-by-three grid in order to re-create the Master Photo.
4. After the group has decided on their solution, email everyone the Master Photo to compare with their solution.

Variations

This is a great game for a team to experience a second time during the duration of their project. For example, you could first use the game in the storming stage, then again in the performing stage to help a team recognize their improvement regarding communication and problem solving. Two different grids are available online so you can use a different photo each time.

Discussion Questions

1. What were some of the challenges you experienced as a team?
2. Did you have a strategy for coming to a decision as a team? If so, how effective was it?
3. Did you experience any conflict as you worked toward a solution? If so, how did you deal with it?
4. Is there anything you would do differently if you were to repeat this challenge?
5. What did you learn from this process about making decisions and creating consensus as a team?

Haiku

OBJECTIVES

- To have team members creatively describe themselves or the team
- To stretch comfort zones
- To explore ways of communicating clearly and

Team Size
Any

Materials
None

Time
10 to 15 minutes

Technology
Online collaborative tool or team website, conference call

DISTANCE SEPARATES
CONNECTED BY OUR PURPOSE
WE WORK TOGETHER

Procedure

Prior to your team conference call, email the haiku instructions to team members and request that they create a personal haiku to share during the call.

- Haiku is a Japanese style of poem.
- Haiku have three lines.
- The first and last lines have five syllables.
- The second line contains seven syllables.
- Haiku do not usually rhyme.

During your conference call, have team members read their haiku to the team. If you wish, post the completed haiku on your online collaborative tool or your team website.

Variations

This can be used at any stage of group development. If used in the forming stage, have team members describe themselves; during the performing stage, have them (in small groups) describe their team; during the transforming stage, have them describe what they appreciated or valued about being part of the team.

Discussion Questions

1. How did you feel about sharing your haiku? Did you stretch your comfort zone?
2. What communication lessons can we learn from the structure of a haiku?
3. Building structure into email can improve consistency on a virtual team. What are some ways we can structure our emails to each other?
4. How does an activity like this help develop trust?
5. What are some other ways that trust is developed on a virtual team?

Hear Ye

OBJECTIVES

- To understand the benefits of effective listening
- To experience disagreement and work through it with a team member

Team Size

Any; team members work with partners

Materials

Hear Ye Listening Test (provided here, and available for download from virtualteambuildinggames.com)

Time

30 minutes

Technology

Email, phone, conference call for discussion questions

Procedure

The team members will be taking a test to assess their listening skills. First, have team members form partnerships. Email the Listening Test to team members and request they individually take five minutes to answer true or false for each of the twenty statements. The next step is to discuss their answers with their partner. They will need to arrange a time to have a conversation with their partner before the next team meeting to discuss their answers and come to consensus. Any area of disagreement is to be thoroughly discussed to gain a clear understanding of each partner's position. At the start of your next team meeting, debrief using the discussion questions.

A special thank you to Carol Tuffahah for this game.

Discussion Questions

1. What did you learn about listening?
2. Did you and your partner agree on all 20 questions?
3. While this test was primarily about listening, there is also a "dealing with conflict" component. How did you deal with disagreements?
4. While reviewing your answers, did you spend more time on areas of agreement or disagreement? Why?
5. What techniques did you use to gain a clear understanding of your partner's perspective?
6. How do we benefit when team members have different opinions, perspectives, and ideas?
7. How can we promote the sharing of differing opinions?
8. What can you do to become a better listener?

GET IT ONLINE!

Hear Ye Listening Test

What do you know about listening?

Please print and complete this listening test before your conversation with your partner. Answer true or false for each of the twenty items in this list. Discuss in detail any areas of disagreement.

_________ **1.** People who get the facts right are always good listeners.

_________ **2.** Listening involves more than your ears.

_________ **3.** Hearing is the same as listening.

_________ **4.** Skill in listening improves your self-confidence.

_________ **5.** Good listening comes naturally when we pay attention.

_________ **6.** You can listen well and do other things at the same time.

_________ **7.** Posture affects listening.

_________ **8.** Most listening distractions can be controlled.

_________ **9.** If you can't remember something, you weren't really listening.

_________ **10.** Good listeners are usually more efficient in completing their work.

_________ **11.** Good listeners never interrupt.

_________ **12.** People like you when you listen to them.

GET IT ONLINE!

__________ **13.** Listening is a passive activity.

__________ **14.** Careful listening helps to settle disagreements before they get bigger.

__________ **15.** Intelligent responses are easier when you listen.

__________ **16.** I make most of my decisions independently rather than by listening to the opinions of others.

__________ **17.** Learning to listen to customers and clients helps you respond more quickly to their needs.

__________ **18.** Few good listeners are promoted to top management positions.

__________ **19.** Good listeners are not often embarrassed by unnecessary mistakes.

__________ **20.** Handling distractions is difficult for good listeners.

Line Up

OBJECTIVES

- To improve communication
- To learn about the other members of the team
- To problem-solve as a team

Team Size
6 to 12

Materials
Line Up list of categories (provided here, and available for download from virtualteambuildinggames.com)

Time
10 to 20 minutes

Technology
Online collaborative tool, conference call

1.Anna January 20
2.Ben February 10
3.Carlos March 4
4.Dante March 5
5.Erin April 24
6.
7.
8.
9.

Procedure

This is a good game for the beginning of your storming stage. You are introducing problem solving and a small amount of conflict for your team to work through.

Open the online collaborative document and type a list of numbers equal to the number of people on your team. Tell the team you will be calling out a category, and they have to "line up" in order, based on the category. Each person places themselves on the list and moves themselves as necessary. Each team member can *only* place and move him- or herself. The easiest way to explain the game is to call out the first category: line up in order of birthdays—the year doesn't matter, just the month and day you were born. The list will look like this:

1. Anika February 22
2. Elaine March 18

3. Josef May 1
4. Jamal May 2
5. Rafael July 14
6. Katrina August 31
7. Lucas September 5
8. Rob December 19

If the team discovers that someone is in the wrong order, the whole team is affected and each person is required to change his or her own position.

Tips

This game is a great lead-in to the Communication Best Practices activity (page 95).

Variations

You can make this more challenging by making it a timed event. Using the first category (birthdays) as your base time, challenge the team to improve with each subsequent category. Allow planning time after the first round.

Discussion Questions

1. Was this challenge difficult for the team? Why or why not?
2. How did you organize yourselves to achieve your goal?
3. What did you learn from this activity that will be helpful to your virtual team?

GET IT ONLINE!

Line Up

Examples of categories:

- Birthdays
- Number of pets
- Number of past jobs
- Number of children
- Number of siblings
- Shoe size
- Length of hair
- Height
- Number of pieces of jewelry that you are wearing right now (including watch)
- Length of time at current company
- Number of books in your personal library
- Number of times you have cried at the movies
- Alphabetical order in order of your middle name
- Alphabetical order in order of your birthplace
- Alphabetical order in order of your mother or father's first name

Logic Puzzler

OBJECTIVES
- To sharpen verbal communication skills
- To problem solve and reach a decision as a team

Team Size
Any

Materials
Logic Puzzler Clues (provided here, and available for download at virtualteambuildinggames.com)

Time
20 to 30 minutes

Technology
Email, conference call

Procedure

This puzzle is designed to engage a group's verbal communication and problem-solving skills. Members are challenged to work out the solution as a team, without using pencil and paper, relying only on discussion and verbal communication to solve the puzzle.

1. Split large teams into smaller problem-solving groups of four to eight team members.
2. Email one of the eight Logic Puzzler Clues to each of the eight different members of your team. If you have fewer than eight people on your team, distribute the clues as evenly as possible, making sure everyone gets at least one clue.
3. Using verbal communication only (no writing, drawing, or doodling allowed!), see if your team can solve this puzzle: Four friends are spending a weekend in the great outdoors. Each person enjoys a different activity and each prefers

a different beverage. Using the clues provided, can you determine who enjoys each activity and which beverage each prefers?

Discussion Questions

1. How did this challenge you as a team?
2. Was there a plan prior to starting?
3. How did you deal with the inability to write anything down?
4. What roles did team members play?
5. How easy or difficult was it to reach a decision as a team? Why?
6. How can we apply these ideas to our virtual team?

GET IT ONLINE!

Logic Puzzler Clues

1. Kristen is not a coffee drinker.
2. The person who is hiking likes orange juice.
3. Mitch doesn't like tea.
4. Angela is not swimming.
5. Rusty doesn't like root beer.
6. Kristen is a mountain biker.
7. The person who prefers coffee is not swimming.
8. Mitch is fishing.

Solution

Kristen, mountain biking, root beer
Mitch, fishing, coffee
Angela, hiking, orange juice
Rusty, swimming, tea

Open Water

OBJECTIVES

- To improve communication
- To foster working together as a team to achieve a task

Team Size

Up to 8

Materials

Images of life raft inventory (provided here, and available for download from virtualteambuilding games.com)

Time

10 to 15 minutes

Technology

Phone, email, online meeting software (optional)

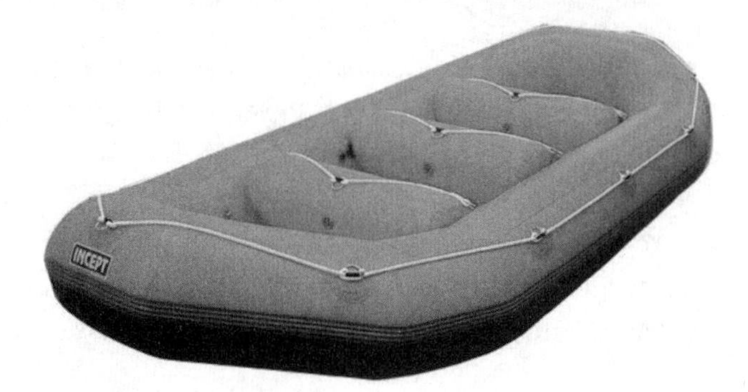

Procedure

This activity requires some preparation on the game leader's part, but the activity provides many opportunities to engage in productive debate, learn how to leverage one another's knowledge, and experience the benefits of collaboration.

Scenario: Your team has escaped a sinking ship by setting out on a life raft that will hold up to eight people. You look around and see that you are in the middle of the ocean with land nowhere in sight. You have a limited inventory of items on board your raft that may be helpful. In addition, each team member had just enough time to grab one personal item before the ship went down. Using all the available resources, your team must work together to survive for as long as possible with the goal of being rescued.

Preparation: Have each team member think about one important item he or she would bring on a cruise. Do not give details about the scenario at this point as it will affect the item each team member chooses to bring. Invite the team members to think creatively and send you a photo or image of the item they selected. Encourage team members to send a photo of something they own for a more personal approach to the activity. Create three PowerPoint slides or shared online documents:

- **Slide 1:** Create a slide titled "The Scenario" that includes the images of all the life-raft inventory, provided at the end of this game (and on the book's website), as well as the following text:

  You are strangers who are the only survivors of a ship that has just sunk. You escaped on a life raft big enough to hold eight people. The life raft has the following items on board, which you may use however you choose:

  - 100 yards of fishing line with no hook
  - flashlight with 24 hours of battery power
  - 50 feet of rope
  - 3-hour flare
  - one oar
  - empty water bladder

- **Slide 2:** Create a slide titled "Equipment on Hand" that includes the images of the team members' selected items, as well as the following text:

  Each of you has also brought specific items with you on the ship, which you grabbed before getting into the life raft. You are all wearing Hawaiian shirts, shorts, and sneakers. Other than your clothing and the one item you brought, you have nothing else.

- **Slide 3:** Create a slide titled "Find Solutions" that includes the following text: Brainstorm how you can combine the equipment you have to survive the longest. To use any piece of equipment you must say the name of the owner when referencing it, for example, "Mike's rope," "Lily's belt," "Nico's knife," and so on. To increase your likelihood for rescue you need (1) fresh water, (2) a method to signal rescuers, and (3) food.

This activity can be conducted via email and phone, but will work much better if you can do it live using online meeting software. Present the slides the first time and then give control of the presentation to someone else on the team, who will move back and forth between the slides, as needed. Watch the time and encourage creativity. Remind them of the rule that they must name the owner of the equipment in order to use that piece of equipment.

Discussion Questions

1. What was the most important item that someone brought?
2. What proved to be the most effective skill in coming up with workable solutions?
3. Do you feel everyone's voice was heard in coming up with potential solutions?
    a. If yes, what did the team do to encourage everyone's input?
    b. If no, what could have been done to increase the level of input?
4. How does this activity mirror our own team and the skills each person brings?

GET IT ONLINE!

Images of Life Raft Inventory

Plus Deltas

OBJECTIVES

- To quickly gather team feedback
- To encourage honest, meaningful feedback

Team Size
Up to 12

Materials
None

Time
10 minutes

Technology
Conference call, online collaborative tool

+	Δ
• Great interaction	• More time for questions
• Like problem solving	• Need minutes prior
• Lots of team involvement	• Discussion time too short
• Agenda is very helpful	• Specific objectives
• Ideas for communication	• Missing resources

Procedure

This activity gives teams a framework for providing honest, meaningful feedback to any process. Use it after a meeting, training session, or project milestone to gather feedback that is framed in a positive way. Using the online collaborative tool, the leader will create two columns. Label the column on the left with the + (plus) symbol as the header, and label the column on the right with a triangle shape, also known as "delta." Tell the team that the "+" column is for documenting things that went well. The column with the triangle symbol is for documenting things that should be changed.

Explain the importance of getting critical, meaningful feedback. Encourage team members to share what they honestly think. Along the way, determine if you are getting enough critical feedback. If you feel you are not getting enough critical feedback, then you may choose to close out the list of "things going well" and only accept items related to "things needing to be changed."

The leader should ask these two questions:

1. What are some things that went really well? (Write these under the + symbol.)
2. What are some things that should be changed? (Write these under the delta or triangle symbol.)

Ensure that everyone on the team has the opportunity to share at least one item that went well or should be changed.

Discussion Questions

1. How comfortable are you giving critical feedback about a project, meeting, training, or any activity we are engaged in?
2. What are some barriers to people giving critical, meaningful feedback?
3. What is the impact on the team if all of us refrain from providing critical, meaningful feedback?
4. What can we do to encourage authentic feedback?

Rat-a-Tat-Tat

OBJECTIVES

- To understand how our perspective can get in the way of clear communication
- To become aware of the benefits of being open-minded

Team Size

Any; team members work with partners

Materials

Instructions (provided here, and available for download from virtualteambuildinggames.com)

Time

5 to 10 minutes

Technology

Phone; conference call for team debriefing discussion

Procedure

Have team members work in pairs. While on the phone, each partner will tap out a simple song on his or her desktop for less than 30 seconds while the other person listens.

1. Team member one taps out a simple song.
2. Team member two guesses the song.
3. Before team member one confirms or denies the accuracy, team member two taps out a different song.
4. Team member one guesses the song.
5. Both team members can reveal their song.
6. Have the partners discuss the activity before the whole team processes the game.

Discussion Questions

1. How accurate were your guesses?
2. How surprised were you that your partner had such difficulty guessing your song?
3. As you were tapping, did you think that it should be "obvious" to your partner what song you were tapping?
4. Do we ever make similar assumptions when communicating?
5. How do our perceptions get in the way of communication?
6. How might this lead to conflict?
7. What's the solution?

Smashing Obstacles

OBJECTIVES

- To improve the way the team communicates
- To understand the obstacles inherent to virtual meetings
- To discover solutions to overcoming those obstacles

Team Size
Any

Materials
None

Time
30 minutes

Technology
Conference call

Procedure

Split the team into smaller discussion groups of three or four people.

Challenge each group to brainstorm a list of potential obstacles to working together virtually during the lifetime of the team. Assign each group a different theme.

Examples of assignments:

- Email
- Conference calls
- Working from different time zones
- Technology
- Online meetings

Group tasks:

1. For each obstacle, have them come up with one or more solutions.
2. Ask each group to come up with two or three discussion questions.
3. Each group can present their findings to the entire team, using questions to prompt discussion.

Tips

Sequence this game sometime before the Communication Best Practices activity (page 95).

Variations

This can be adapted for a time-dispersed team using an online collaborative tool to brainstorm and present findings.

Discussion Questions

The discussion questions will be developed by each group and will be part of the presentation.

Tuned Out

OBJECTIVES

- To experience how our feedback influences communication
- To discover how multitasking impacts listening

Team Size

Any; team members work with partners

Materials

None

Time

10 to 15 minutes

Technology

Email, phone

Procedure

Team members work with partners for this game. Email the rules along with partner assignments and request that before the next team meeting, they take 10 minutes to play the game and answer the questions. Debrief the entire team at the beginning of your next meeting.

Instructions

Taking turns, partners tell each other a story about themselves. The story could be about a memorable vacation, an interesting story from their past, or some recent experience.

1. As one partner tells a story, the other partner listens, offers feedback, acknowledges understanding, and asks questions to clarify.
2. At some point in the conversation, the listener should read an email while listening to the talker's story. The talker should see if he or she is able to guess when the listener has started to multitask.
3. Once the talker is done with his or her story, the listener retells the talker's story, and the talker evaluates how well the listener listened.

4. The partners switch roles and the listener becomes the talker, and the talker becomes the listener. Again, the new listener must at some point read an email while continuing to give feedback and ask questions.
5. Once the talker is done, the listener retells the story, and the talker evaluates how well the listener listened.
6. The talkers share whether they were able to tell when the other person began multitasking.

Discussion Questions

1. How accurate were you in guessing the exact moment your listener tuned out?
2. How common is it to multitask while on the phone?
3. How does this impact our communication?
4. In what ways could this lead to conflict?
5. How does this fit in with our norms or "Team Communication Best Practices"?

Virtual High Fives

OBJECTIVES

- To creatively solve a problem as a team
- To improve communication skills

Team Size

Any

Materials

Digital camera or webcam

Time

10 to 15 minutes

Technology

Shared online document

Procedure

This is a fun challenge for the beginning of the storming stage of group development. Tell the team that their goal is to create a set of action photos that depict team members interacting in a physical way, even though they are separated. Team members can form partnerships, small groups, or the whole team can work together. The only requirement is that two or more people are interacting in the photo. For example: two team members giving each other a high five; two people shaking hands; one person pouring coffee into another person's mug; team members spelling something by using their hands and bodies, such as "YMCA." Use a shared online document that allows you to upload and paste photos such as Google docs. Position your photos in the document side by side or resize the photos to make the action appear as realistic as possible.

Post all photos on the team website.

Tips

Play this a few times during the duration of your virtual team, encouraging new partnerships, and to assess process improvement.

Discussion Questions

1. What are some challenges of not being face to face?
2. What are some challenges a virtual team may experience that a traditional team may not?
3. How did you work through your challenges in this game?
4. How can you apply this to your virtual team?

3

Virtual Team-Building Games for the Norming Stage

Interdependent people combine their own efforts with the efforts of others to achieve their greatest success.

—*Steven Covey*

The Norming Stage

Cooperation and trust are now becoming the "norm" for the team. The team begins to better understand the respective personalities of other team members so the diverse perspectives can come together to work more effectively. Team members should also have a good understanding of which technology is preferred and most efficient to interact with other team members.

Good things are starting to happen, and as a result, the team feels more confident, connected, and creative. The team looks to the leader for support during this stage. Team members can take leadership roles by facilitating games from this chapter.

BVTE (Best Virtual Team Ever)

OBJECTIVES

- To develop a sense of team spirit
- To understand each team member's responsibility for team success

Team Size
Any

Materials
None

Time
10 to 15 minutes

Technology
Conference call, online collaborative tool; team website

Procedure

Split the team into brainstorming groups of four to six people. Each group will require a scribe and need to set up a group conference call. The scribe needs to access or open the online collaborative document for everyone in the group to see during the brainstorming session. Remind the team the of rules for brainstorming:

- Note each idea.
- Do not discuss or evaluate ideas.
- The goal is quantity, not quality.

The topic of the brainstorming is: Think about our virtual team. What can we do to make our team the best virtual team ever (BVTE)?

Each group's scribe should write down as many ideas as possible. After two minutes, ask the groups to refine their ideas before submitting them to the team for negotiation. The ideas submitted have to be clear, specific, and stated in a positive manner (what to do rather than what *not* to do). The facilitator then gathers all of the ideas so everyone can see them. Let the team know that the norms they create will be observed and exhibited by the team for the duration of the project. Make sure the team defines any terms that may be open to interpretation. For example, what does "be accountable" mean?

Tips

Post the team norms on a team website and periodically check on the agreements to determine how well the team is following its own code of conduct. The team can add, modify, and evaluate as necessary.

Variations

A funny variation is to flip this activity on its head and have the team brainstorm around what it takes to be the worst virtual team ever (WVTE). The ideas generated can then be flipped to create positive norms for the team.

Discussion Questions

1. How does it benefit a team to have a code of conduct?
2. What are some ways we can work together to make this the BVTE?
3. How can we hold each other accountable?
4. How would we like to receive feedback?

Conference Call Bingo

OBJECTIVES

- To add fun to your team meeting
- To encourage active listening and reduce multitasking during virtual meetings

Team Size
Up to 20

Materials
Conference Call Bingo Card (provided here, and available for download from virtualteambuildinggames.com), Pen

Time
The length of your scheduled meeting

Technology
Conference call, email

B	I	N	G	O
		X		

Procedure

Using the template provided, assign a different team member the job of Bingo scorekeeper during your meetings.

When the scorekeeper hears a specific phrase or action, he or she should place a checkmark in that spot on the Bingo card. The scorekeeper may mark the same space several times. At the end of your meeting, be sure to allow time for the scorekeeper to report the results to your team.

Variations

You can change any of the squares to tailor the game for your team.

Discussion Questions

1. Which phrases or actions were marked most frequently?
2. What is the impact on our meeting when we do these things more frequently?

GET IT ONLINE!

Conference Call Bingo Card

B	I	N	G	O
Speak clearly	Assign roles to team members	Give everyone a chance to talk	Eliminate side conversations	Take roll call before starting the discussion
Use names	Ask clarifying questions	Ask for feedback	Include an icebreaker or climate-setting activity	Take ownership
Stick to agenda	Have an agenda	Take a leadership role	Set objectives	Assign action items
Examine the meeting process	Review the process for improvements	Listen without interrupting	Keep background noise to a minimum	Take turns speaking
Show recognition	Provide specific feedback	Start on time	End on time	Have everyone introduce themselves
When you speak, use your name to identify yourself	Keep the tone light with appropriate use of humor	Close the meeting by thanking everyone for their time	Close with clear next steps	Send the dial-in number, passcode, and instructions multiple times

End on a High Note

OBJECTIVES

- To end meetings on a high note
- To motivate one another
- To verbalize appreciation for another team member

Team Size
Any

Materials
None

Time
5 minutes

Technology
Conference call

Procedure

Before disconnecting your conference call at the end of your next meeting, allow a few minutes for team members to provide praise for others who have helped them out during the past week or performed some action worthy of recognition. The first time, be prepared with your own praise and recognition to get the process started. Doing this at the conclusion of each meeting allows you to end on a high note and gain the attention of everyone on the call. Create a name for this part of your meetings. To get the team prepared, you can even hold a contest for the name! Before you know it, this will be a highly anticipated and routine part of your team meetings. Believe me, the team will let you know if you ever forget this part.

Tips

If your team is time dispersed, you can adapt this idea to notes posted on a team website or online collaborative tool

Variations

Sometimes it is helpful to set the tone at the beginning of a meeting by using this activity then, especially if you know the meeting will be challenging in nature and you want to foster a more positive approach.

Discussion Questions

No discussion questions are necessary.

Job Description

OBJECTIVES

- To clarify team roles and expectations
- To brainstorm the key success factors for team members

Team Size
Any

Materials
None

Time
10 to 20 minutes

Technology
Email, conference call, online collaborative tool or team website

JOB DESCRIPTION

Role:
Teammember

Competencies:
1. *Communicator*
2. *Date driven*
3. *Creative*
4. *Brings donuts!*
5. *Team-focused*

Procedure

This brainstorming activity helps your team identify the qualities, characteristics, and behaviors that the ideal team member would possess. To achieve this, the team will develop a job description for the role of a team member. This is especially helpful if you are still building the team or may have new team members joining at later phases.

Email the team beforehand and ask that each team member come prepared with a list of five competencies that are required for a team member to be successful on this team. Have the team members share their five competencies at the meeting, and then refine the list to include whatever the team feels is essential. Encourage everyone to discuss and debate their ideas before choosing the team's top five competencies.

As you create your job descriptions, focus on collecting the key ideas and competencies that will make a person successful in this role. Don't worry about perfect phrasing, just focus on gathering ideas. In doing this you are also setting norms and describing behaviors you expect from each other. Once complete, share the job description with the team on your team website or online collaborative tool.

Discussion Questions

1. Why are these competencies important for a team member to have?
2. What is an acceptable way to hold each other accountable for these competencies?
3. If a team member joined our team and did not exhibit these characteristics and behaviors, what would be the impact?
4. Do we feel we are lacking in any of these competencies on our team? If so, how can we develop them?

Same but Different

OBJECTIVES

- To sharpen communication skills
- To experience team problem solving

Team Size

Up to 12

Materials

Same but Different pictures (available for download from virtualteambuildinggames.com)

Time

25 to 30 minutes

Technology

Email, conference call

Procedure

Distribute via email the provided Same but Different pictures to your team members. Each picture will get sent to two team members. If you have an odd number of team members, one person can listen as an observer, making sure to take notes to add to his or her perspective to the debriefing discussion.

Via conference call, the team members must find the one and only partner who has the exact same picture. This is done in real time on the call; emailing the picture is not allowed. Although each image initially looks the same, team members will discover that there are small details that differ between pictures. Team members must discover how to communicate effectively to describe their pictures and find their partners.

Tips

This activity is a fun way to have team members partner up for one-on-one discussions.

Discussion Questions

1. How did this challenge you as a team?
2. What communication obstacles did you encounter?
3. What strategy did your team use to sort through all the pictures? Was it successful? Would you use a different approach if you were to do this again?
4. Did anyone play a leadership role? If so, was a leader selected by the team, or did a leader emerge during the course of the activity?

Secret Coach

OBJECTIVES

- To provide positive feedback to another team member
- To maintain a high level of engagement during team meetings

Team Size

Any

Materials

None

Time

This activity will be integrated into your team meeting, with no additional time required

Technology

Conference call

Procedure

Randomly assign each team member to act as a coach to another team member. The coach's job is to encourage, support, and recognize his or her "coachee" during the team meeting without that person discovering who his or her personal coach is.

Tips

This activity can be incorporated into more than one meeting. Played early on in your team's formation, this game can create meeting norms regarding feedback, engagement, and positive communication.

Variations

If your team is time dispersed, you can adapt this idea to notes posted on a team website or online collaborative tool.

Discussion Questions

1. Coaches: How did your role as coach impact your participation?
2. In what ways did it affect the way you listened?
3. Others: How did it feel to have someone "have your back" during the meeting?
4. How did this impact the team dynamic?
5. In what ways does this benefit the team?

Team Status Updates

OBJECTIVES

- To get to know each other
- To foster team trust

Team Size
Any

Materials
None

Time
1 minute per team member

Technology
Conference call, online collaborative tool (optional)

Procedure

Popular social networking tools such as Facebook and Google+ encourage friends to share what is on their mind in very brief status updates. These status updates may be written words, images, videos, or songs. For this activity, each team member will provide a status update to share his or her feelings about the team or the project they are working on. Other team members may choose to "Like" someone else's status update if they have shared something that resonates with them.

Prior to a scheduled meeting, the leader will ask each participant to prepare a brief "status update" as if they were posting it on Facebook or Google+. Each team member will state his or her status update with the rest of the team during the call. Encourage team members to follow the "bulletin board" rule. In most organizations, the "bulletin board" rule means do not write anything that you would not be comfortable sharing via a bulletin board in a busy hallway at work. The leader should give each participant a moment to share his or her status update with the group. If team members share something visual, they can describe what the visual is to the group. If your meeting is online, you can have each team member share his or her screen briefly so everyone may see the visual being shared.

Variations

Encourage team members to request status updates from everyone whenever they are unsure or unclear about the current climate of the team. Team members can simply open a document in the online collaborative tool, head the document with a phrase such as "How is everyone doing?" or "Status update, please," add their update, and share it with everyone on the team.

Discussion Questions

1. How did your status reflect your feelings about the project?
2. Of all the statuses that were shared, are there any you would "Like" because it resonates with you as well? Which one(s)?
3. Do you see any trends in the statuses that were shared?

Team Story

OBJECTIVES

- To understand the value of seeing the big picture
- To experience the confusion that threaded conversations may impose

Team Size
7 to 12

Materials
Team Story instructions (provided here and available for download from virtualteambuildinggames.com.)

Time
10 to 20 minutes

Technology
Email, conference call

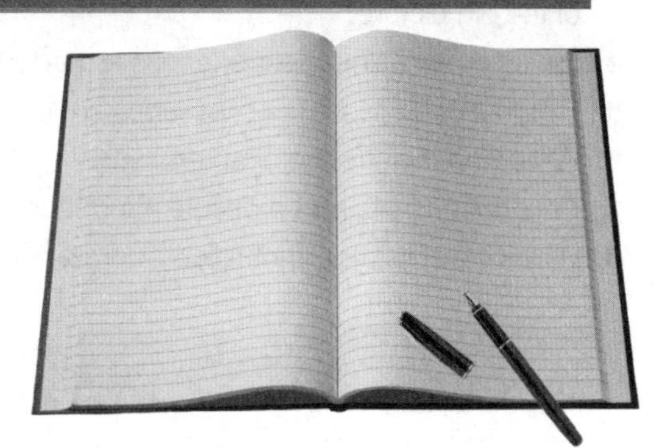

Procedure

Send an email to one person on your team.

1. Instruct one person on the team to write one sentence and then email "The Story" thread to another person.
2. The Story thread is then emailed to the next team member, who must add one additional sentence and his or her name to the list, then email it to the next person.
3. Team members can count the sentences to judge where they are in the process.
4. This process is repeated until everyone on the team has added a sentence to The Story.
5. No additional discussion is permitted pertaining to the message or its meaning. Nor may team members ask questions to gain clarification or perspective.

6. Upon completion of the message, the last person can read the team's completed story to the entire group for their mutual enjoyment.

Discussion Questions

1. What were your challenges along the way?
2. How easy was the understanding between team members?
3. In what ways does it benefit the team when each team member has an idea of the big picture?
4. Have you had similar experiences regarded threaded conversations?
5. How can we ensure our messages are clear to our recipients?
6. What was the effect of time pressure?
7. How does stress and pressure affect our willingness to collaborate?
8. Why may it be important to collaborate during times of stress and pressure?

GET IT ONLINE!

Cut and paste this information before resending:

Please add one sentence to this story and email these instructions along with "The Story" to any other person on the team. Each team member should receive the message once. If there is no first sentence for The Story following these instructions, you are the first person, therefore your task it to start the process with a topic sentence of your choosing. Remember to add your name to the list of names at the bottom so we can track who has yet to add their sentence.

The Story

(Please add your sentence to complete our team's story)

Team members' names:

1. ______________________________

2. ______________________________

3. ______________________________

4. ______________________________

5. ______________________________

6. ______________________________

7. ______________________________

Team Teach

OBJECTIVES

- To give team members an opportunity to take a leadership role
- To allow team members to practice running a team meeting
- To reveal something team members are passionate about or good at

Team Size
Any

Materials
None

Time
10 to 20 minutes

Technology
Online meeting software

Procedure

This activity is twofold: For teams with a number of newcomers to virtual meetings, team members will learn skills to help them take a leadership role and even run a virtual meeting. For teams more versed in virtual meetings, this game is a chance for team members to share something they are good at. Each team member will lead a short virtual team meeting where they will be required to teach the team a skill. The topic of the meeting could be anything from cooking a certain dish to effective email skills. Select a different team member each month to conduct a session.

The team member needs to:

- Create an agenda
- Run the meeting
- Determine any follow-up needed

Encourage meeting leaders to use images, slides, graphics, video, or anything else that will help them present their topic more clearly.

Discussion Questions

No discussion questions are necessary.

Tell, Decide, Ignore

OBJECTIVES

- To brainstorm a list of communication methods and select which would be appropriate for the team in specific situations
- To develop a protocol for clarifying the purpose of all team communications

Team Size

Up to 12

Materials

None

Time

20 minutes

Technology

Conference call, online meeting software (optional)

Procedure

There are two parts to this game that leverage the brainstorming abilities of your team. This game reinforces brainstorming techniques while taking that information and applying it immediately to a group challenge.

During a conference call, the leader asks team members to brainstorm a list of methods of communication they might use to ensure that everyone stays in touch with important team updates. The leader should encourage everyone to suggest ideas based on the various methods of communication available to the team. This is especially useful if the team has not documented or agreed upon the standard communication processes for the group. The leader should ask questions to fully explore all the potential communication needs. Here are some sample questions you could use to generate a good list of ideas:

1. What are the various times that we need to communicate with each other? *Possible answers: in an emergency, need to ask a question, need to tell someone something, need a decision made, just an FYI to everyone, seeking feedback, just checking in for an update, publishing information, when is lunch?*
2. What are the various methods we use to do this communication? *Possible answers: desk phone, email, conference call, online meeting, discussion group, Twitter, cell phone, website posting, instant messenger*

As the group brainstorms the different reasons for communication, the leader organizes the ideas into three to five major categories such as:

- Seeking feedback
- Seeking decision
- Seeking update
- Publishing info
- Relationship building

The leader asks the team the following questions, giving them time to respond to each:

1. Have you ever received an email from someone, read it, and afterward were unclear what the original purpose for sending the email was? Tell us what went through your head after reading it. *Possible responses: waste of time, filling my email, confusing, what's the point?*
2. Have you ever sent an email, expecting feedback or a decision, but you receive no response at all? Tell us what went through your head after receiving the wrong response. *Possible responses: frustration, feeling ignored, have to resend my email, escalate to the recipient's boss, waste of my time*

The leader should confirm for the group that everyone has probably felt these same feelings at some point. Explain that high-performing teams find ways to easily communicate with one another the specific purpose of each message. Keeping that in mind, ask the team, "What are some ways we could clarify the purpose of each of our communications to ensure we get what we need?"

Suggested ideas for message clarity and consistency:

- Use a code word in the email subject line such as INFO, DECISION, FYI, FEEDBACK.
- At the beginning of the message, clearly and briefly state the purpose of the communication. For example, "Looking for a decision by Tuesday."

Your team will create their own language and process for communicating purpose and expectations. This activity helps to establish communication norms to increase your team's ability to be effective and efficient. The outcome will be clearer communication and an increase in appropriate responses.

Discussion Questions

No discussion questions are necessary.

Ten for 10

OBJECTIVES

- To place focus on continuous improvement
- To discover more effective ways to work together
- To empower the team to discover breakthroughs and efficiencies regarding the team's processes

Team Size

Any

Materials

"Ten for 10" questions (provided here, and available for download from virtualteambuildinggames.com)

Time

10 minutes

Technology

Conference call, team website or online collaborative tool

TEN *for* 10

Procedure

This game provides a great way to empower your team to discover inefficiencies and then create solutions regarding the team's processes. To introduce the idea to your team, post the 10 questions during a team meeting. Let the team know you are committed to helping them work smarter, not harder. To that end, you would like them to consider the 10 questions throughout their workday.

During team meetings, address some of the ways the team can improve their processes based on the 10 questions. The idea is to make it a regular part of your meetings to take ten minutes for the 10 questions. For example, one team member may have been frustrated with his or her Internet connection. When the team member tried to send a file, it was bounced back because the file was too large. What's the solution? The objective is not to create a gripe session in your meetings, but to empower the team to look for solutions by sharing the issues they encounter in their day.

Display the 10 questions prominently to demonstrate your commitment to process improvement. Post the questions on your team website or online collaborative tool. In addition, ask team members to display the questions in their work space to remind them that everyone on the team needs to focus on the details for the team to be successful.

Creating a norm around the 10 questions promotes a higher level of commitment to excellence as well as a greater awareness of any issues that prevent team members from doing their best. Increase the level of accountability by having the team create the norms regarding how the team will use "Ten for 10."

Here are some examples:

- We take ten minutes periodically throughout our day/week to answer the 10 questions.
- We take ten minutes during meetings to discover breakthroughs based on the answers to the 10 questions.
- When things don't go as planned, we take a moment to reflect on the 10 questions and how they may have played a part and how to use the questions to learn from the situation.
- We regularly check in to answer the 10 questions.

Tips

Have different team members facilitate the "Ten for 10" portion of your team meetings.

Variations

Have your team members come up with their own 10 questions.

Discussion Questions

The discussion questions will be based on the answers to the questions.

GET IT ONLINE!

Ten for 10

1. What frustrated you today?
2. What took too long?
3. What caused complaints?
4. What was misunderstood?
5. What cost too much?
6. What was wasted?
7. What was too complicated?
8. What was just plain silly?
9. What took too many people?
10. What job involved too many steps?

Un-Virtually Yours

OBJECTIVES

- To foster communication
- To learn more about each other

Team Size

Any

Materials

A small- to medium-size box for shipping; fun, creative, interesting, or thought-provoking items provided by the team members

Time

Short periods of time over the course of a month

Technology

Conference call, digital camera, traditional mailing or shipping service, online collaborative tool or team website

Procedure

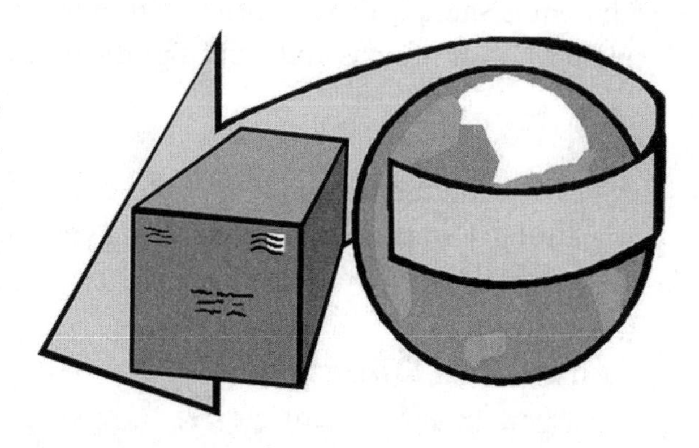

In this activity, each team member will receive a small box in the mail with an item in it. He or she will remove the item and replace it with another item. The box will then be mailed to the next specified team member. Request that team members take a creative approach to the game, and encourage the team to send fun and interesting items. During the debriefing discussion, each team member will have a chance to articulate why the item was chosen.

To prepare for this activity, the facilitator should create a list of team members and their mailing addresses. This list will be shared with the team members when the instructions are given as to how to do this activity. Team members need to be instructed to mail the box to the next person on the list and not skip anyone.

Depending on the size of your team, this activity could take days or weeks to complete. The box continues being mailed until it reaches the last person, who sends it back to the facilitator. Once the facilitator receives the box, he or she will inform the team that the box has come full circle and will schedule a time to discuss what each team member found in the box. If your organization has interoffice mail, use that process instead. This activity works well with international teams as well. Be sure to remind team members to only include items that can be legally shipped via mail and that nothing fragile should be included.

The facilitator can schedule time at the next conference call to discuss what each team member found in the box. Use the mailing list of team members to debrief this activity in the same order the box was mailed out. One by one have each team member describe the item received in the box, but not the item he or she placed in the box. The next team member will share what was placed in the box. As you hear from the recipients, and each item is shared, also have the team member who placed it in the box explain what the item is and what significance it has for him or her.

Tips

Have each team member take a photo of the item that was received and present it back to the team online using your online collaborative tool or team website during the debriefing discussion.

Discussion Questions

1. What was the funniest item found in the box?
2. What was the most surprising item found in the box?
3. If you could trade your item for any other item in the group, which would you pick?

Virtual Dessert

OBJECTIVES

- To learn more about each other
- To improve facilitation skills in an online meeting
- To incorporate some fun into a team meeting

Team Size
Any

Materials
PowerPoint slide

Time
2 minutes

Technology
Online meeting software, conference call

Procedure

This is a fun, fast activity to bring levity to any meeting, while also providing a small opportunity to learn something about fellow team members. This activity can provide an easy opportunity for team members to share in front of the group and practice using the online meeting tool for facilitation.

The facilitator preselects one team member and asks him or her to find an image of a favorite dessert. The team member should put that image on a slide and present that slide to the team while online during the scheduled meeting. The facilitator will give presentation control over to the selected team member to present his or her virtual dessert. The team member should share why this is a favorite dessert.

Prior to the meeting, make sure the team member is prepared to take over presentation mode for the online meeting. The facilitator may also

---

Special thanks to Allison McDowell, Chief Human Resource Officer at Banner Ironwood Medical Center, for this game.

choose to have the virtual dessert presented at any point in the meeting, not just at the beginning or end. It's a good way to introduce humor and interactivity.

Discussion Questions

No discussion questions are necessary.

Virtual Q&A

OBJECTIVES

- To get to know your teammates better
- To start your virtual meeting or conference call on a positive note

Team Size
Any

Materials
Virtual Q&A Questions (provided here, and available for download from virtualteambuildinggames.com)

Time
10 to 20 minutes

Technology
Conference call or online meeting software

Procedure

Start your conference call or virtual meeting by asking one or two light getting-to-know-you questions. Questions can be of a general nature, or more work specific.

Tips

Use some questions from the provided list or have team members generate questions of their own.

Variations

This activity also works well for teams separated by time zones, different work shifts, or other time barriers. Simply email the questions to all the team members and have them post the questions and answers on your team website or shared online document.

Discussion Questions

No discussion questions are necessary.

GET IT ONLINE!

Virtual Q&A Questions

- Can you describe a memorable meal?
- What is a sport you love to play?
- Who is someone you admire?
- What would be the best place to live?
- What is your favorite candy?
- What are some foods that you cook?
- What would be your fantasy vacation?
- Where did you grow up?
- What is your favorite board game?
- What do you consider the most beautiful beach?
- What season of year do you love the most?
- What is the music you live by?
- What do you consider to be the greatest films of all time?
- What was the worst job you ever had?
- What do you consider to be the finest fast food?
- What is a water activity that you enjoy?
- Who makes you laugh?
- What do you consider the best books of all time?
- What was your favorite childhood toy?
- What is your favorite sport to watch?
- What was your smartest career decision?
- What are two office tools you can't live without?
- Which project have you enjoyed working on the most?
- What business are you a loyal customer of?
- What is an important thing that happened recently?

GET IT ONLINE!

- What is a useful tip for keeping organized?
- If you had a time machine, what one thing you would go back to see?
- What was a strange or funny experience you had at work?
- What do you consider to be valuable traits in a coworker?
- What would be a tough job interview question to ask? to answer?
- What was the first job you ever had?
- What are the primary responsibilities of your position?
- What are the pros and cons of being a leader?
- What is the biggest risk you ever took?
- What two practical skills do you possess?
- What are some ways that you stay motivated or inspired?
- What is a song that you are sure you'll never forget?
- What is your favorite stress buster?
- What is the one item you would never travel without?
- What would be your perfect weekend?
- What is the most interesting biography you have read?
- What would you write a book about?
- What movie/TV show keeps you riveted?
- What was your favorite childhood book?

Where Do You Stand?

OBJECTIVES

- To provide a fast and consistent way for the team to make decisions
- To create buy-in and engagement in the decision-making process

Team Size
Any

Materials
None

Time
2 to 5 minutes

Technology
Conference call

Procedure

Throughout the duration of your virtual team, you will make countless decisions. Distance, silence, and the lack of nonverbal communication can create the illusion that team members are in agreement with a decision when, in fact, they are not. It is easy for someone to disengage when the team is proceeding in a direction a team member disagrees with.

This tool provides a way to determine where the team members stand and if further discussion or information is necessary before making the decision. When you get to the decision-making point, ask your team members to decide where they stand and share their position with the rest of the team using this verbiage:

- "I'm all in"—Confident with decision; can't wait to get started
- "I'm in"—Comfortable with the decision
- "I'm on the line"—Even though I have reservations, I will support the team in this decision
- "I'm dragging my feet"—Don't fully agree, but I won't thwart it
- "I'm out"—Disagree with solution; uncomfortable; require further discussion or information

After everyone has stated their position, it is up to the team or team leader to either encourage further discussion or to move forward with the decision. Establish some team norms regarding the use of this tool.

Tips

Introduce this technique early on after some initial trust-building games. Make it part of your team's norms. Keep in mind that there is a tendency in virtual teams to "go along to get along," so by implementing this tool, you can accurately assess the team's thoughts and feelings before proceeding.

Variations

You can develop your own language for the five different stances to tailor them to your team or industry.

Discussion Questions

1. How does this technique benefit a virtual team?
2. How can we promote inclusion in other areas?
3. To what level are we willing to hold ourselves accountable for providing accurate feedback during this process?

4 Virtual Team-Building Games for the Performing Stage

If everyone is moving forward together, then success takes care of itself.

—*Henry Ford*

The Performing Stage

Here, we're on a roll. The team has momentum, energy, and, ideally, all team members are willing to contribute equally. This is the most productive of all the stages. Tasks are identified and handled efficiently by the members of the team. Individuals respect the contributions of others, and the team is well on its way to meeting and even surpassing its goals and objectives—all the while creating a sense of unity and cohesion. Allow team members to take the lead and facilitate the games in this section. As team leader, be ready to step in if the team experiences storming during this stage. "On a roll" sometimes creates complacency, which can lead to conflict. In addition, the stress involved with deadlines, transitions, and changes can influence the way team members communicate. With their eyes on the goal, they may be more focused on attaining the goal than on interacting with the team. Incorporating a game like Five-Word Snapshot (page 193) or Reality Check (page 207) can be beneficial in the performing stage. Team members have a chance to check in with one another and be heard by the team. Remember that conflict on a team is normal, and by now your team should have some experience and confidence handling conflict. As leader, you can help to mitigate and direct that conflict in a positive and constructive manner. Remember, if everyone always agrees, you may not be hearing from everyone.

A Fresh Point of View

OBJECTIVES

- To discover new ways of thinking about your team's project
- To break out of limiting thoughts and think outside the box

Team Size

Up to 12

Materials

None

Time

20 minutes

Technology

Conference call

Procedure

Sometimes a team can get stuck or limited in the way they see their project. Ask team members to consider the current project they are working on. Now ask them to switch perspectives and look at the project differently based on these ideas:

- Discuss this problem applying a Hollywood movie studio's point of view.
- Discuss this problem applying Apple's approach. Think in terms of attention to design, a pleasing user experience, and so on.
- How would a professional basketball coach approach this project?
- How would a space shuttle crew approach this project?
- How would Albert Einstein approach this project? What ideas would he have?
- What would a five-year-old consider concerning the project?
- Donald Trump?
- Others?

Discussion Questions

1. Was this exercise valuable for our team? In what ways?
2. What can we do differently as a result?
3. How can we ensure that we stay fresh and open to new ways of thinking?

Advanced Virtual Q&A

OBJECTIVES

- To build a deeper level of trust within the team
- To develop closer interpersonal relationships
- To allow team members to reveal personal values

Team Size

Any

Materials

Advanced Virtual Q&A Questions (provided here, and available for download from virtualteambuildinggames.com)

Time

10 to 20 minutes

Technology

Conference call

Procedure

This advanced version of Virtual Q&A deepens the level of self-disclosure and trust among team members. Start your conference call or virtual meeting by asking one or two of these more in-depth questions.

Variations

This activity works well for teams separated by time zones, different work shifts, or other time barriers. Select one or two questions from the list. Email the questions to all the team members and have them reply to all on the distribution list, or post the questions and answers on a team website or shared document.

Discussion Questions

No discussion questions are necessary.

GET IT ONLINE!

Advanced Virtual Q&A Questions

- What one item of clothing are you wearing right now that is most reflective of you?
- If you could improve one personality trait in yourself, what would it be?
- What is one of your superpowers and why?
- What three words would you use to describe yourself?
- What can you do better than anyone else?
- What person in your life has had the greatest impact on you? In what way?
- What is your most compulsive daily ritual?
- What are your pet peeves in the workplace?
- Who was your best role model and why?
- Which of your accomplishments are you most proud of?
- What was the best pet you ever had? Why?
- What is a story that gets told and retold at your family gatherings?
- What was the best advice you ever received? Who gave you that advice?
- What would you do if you knew you would not fail?
- In what way are you superstitious?
- What is the most useful thing you have ever learned?
- What do you like most about your friends?
- What is your biggest time waster?
- What are you an expert at?
- What advice would you give to a friend who has just joined a virtual team?

Count Off

OBJECTIVES
- To problem-solve "on the fly"
- To experience communication challenges and discover ways to overcome them

Team Size
8 to 20
Materials
None
Time
10 to 20 minutes
Technology
Conference call

1
7
5
3
6
8
2
9
4

Procedure
The challenge is for the team to count up to the number of people on the team. For example, a team of ten needs to count from 1 to 10. If two team members speak at the same time, the team starts from the beginning. When this happens, a different person must start the count-off.

Tips
If you have a hybrid team where some team members are on-site and some are remote, a whole different dynamic may occur. Have any team members who are in the same room close their eyes during the game.

Discussion Questions

1. When you first heard the rules for this game, what did you anticipate regarding the difficulty level?
2. Did your experience match your expectations? How was it different?
3. Were you able to multitask during the game? Why or why not?
4. What are some similar situations where it benefits the team to focus our attention?
5. How does this game apply to our work as a virtual team?
6. What did you learn to make you a more effective team member?

DIY

OBJECTIVES

- To tap into the creativity of the team
- To challenge the team

Team Size
Any

Materials
None

Time
20 to 30 minutes

Technology
Various

Procedure

This is best suited for a team in the high-performing stage of team development. By then, team members understand the group dynamic and know each other well enough to know what kind of challenge they are up to.

To begin, split larger teams into small groups of four or five people. Give groups 20 to 30 minutes to come up with a team-building game.

The game needs to follow these guidelines:

- No real-time person-to-person phone calls, conference calls, or VoIP are allowed.
- If online meeting software is used, no audio is allowed.
- If you use email, you have to stick to email only.
- If you use the phone you can only use voice mail; no person-to-person contact is allowed.
- If you use IM, use IM only.

Encourage the group to take advantage of whatever modes of communication your team has available, keeping the guidelines in mind. Tell the groups that the game they develop should require the team to tap into the different elements of teamwork, such as communication, trust, problem solving, and goal setting. Decide ahead of time what time limit you will impose on the games. Anywhere from 10 to 20 minutes is a good guideline to use. In addition, have groups create three discussion questions for their game.

Tips

Encourage creativity and games that stretch the team members' comfort zones. Remind the groups that they will be participating in the game they create, so it's best not to ask another team member to do something they themselves wouldn't do!

Variations

You could feature a different game from each group at the beginning of your team meetings over the course of a couple of weeks.

Discussion Questions

1. How challenging was this activity?
2. Did you experience any conflict?
3. If so, how was it resolved?
4. What team skills did you use to develop your game?
5. Would these same skills be useful for our team?
6. In what ways could we use these same skills to improve our team?

Entrance Music

OBJECTIVES

- To get to know the team members on a more personal level
- To start team meetings in a fun way

Team Size
Any

Materials
None

Time
3 to 5 minutes at the start of your meetings

Technology
Conference call

Procedure

In the performing stage, the team has a clear picture of the team's purpose and is focused on reaching their goal. This is a great time to inject a little fun, and at the same time, provide a way for team members to continue to deepen their relationships. As leader, kick off the idea by beginning a team meeting with a song that has significant meaning for you. Have the music playing as the team joins the call. Make sure all team members hear at least some of the song. After the song is over, explain to the team why you chose the song as your "theme song." Providing an in-depth explanation will set the tone for the rest of the team when it's their turn. Let the team know that a different person will start the team's meetings in the same manner until everyone has had a chance to play his or her song.

As in What's in a Name? game (page 79), you can learn quite a bit about someone else with this low-risk, easy game.

Tips

Send a reminder to the person who is next in line to share his or her music. If sending out an agenda, include the name of the person who will start the meeting with his or her chosen song.

Variations

After hearing everyone's song, have the team choose a theme song for your team.

Discussion Questions

No discussion questions are necessary.

Five-Word Snapshot

OBJECTIVES

- To gain a quick understanding of the group's attitude, feelings, or opinions

Team Size
Up to 20

Materials
None

Time
5 minutes

Technology
Conference call or online collaborative tool

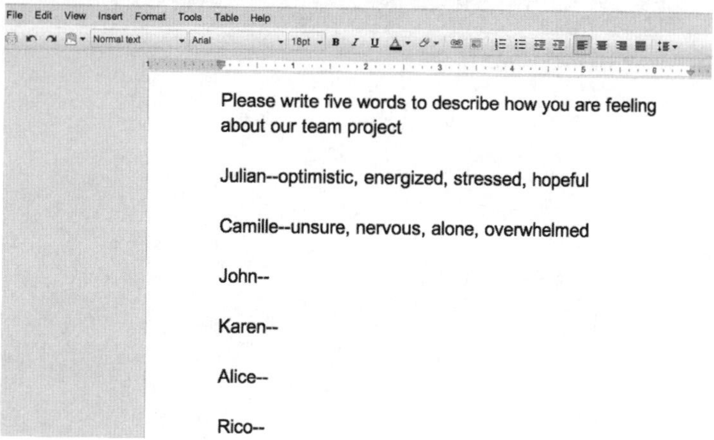
File Edit View Insert Format Tools Table Help
Normal text
Arial
18pt
Please write five words to describe how you are feeling about our team project
Julian--optimistic, energized, stressed, hopeful
Camille--unsure, nervous, alone, overwhelmed
John--
Karen--
Alice--
Rico--

Procedure

This is a simple exercise to get a quick "snapshot view" of the attitudes of your team members. Have them take a few moments to think about how they are feeling at this specific moment about their current work project. Have each person describe his or her feelings or attitude using five words or less. No one else may respond or offer feedback during this exercise; it is simply an opportunity to hear from everyone and gain a quick understanding of where the group stands.

If this activity is done on a conference call, take turns so that everyone gets a chance to speak. If done using an online collaborative tool, have each person type his or her name and five words.

Variations

You can make this anonymous (except to the game leader) by having everyone on the team email their five words to the leader. The leader can cut and paste them into a shared collaborative document for the team to see. The team can then discuss the general feeling of the entire group.

Discussion Questions

1. Why is checking in like this beneficial on a virtual team?
2. Do we usually take the time to do this? Why or why not?
3. What are some outcomes of neglecting to check in?
4. On a traditional team, what are some ways we commonly check the climate of the team? Can we use the same methods virtually?
5. What are some other ways we can discover how team members are feeling?
6. What did you learn?

Flight 287 to Boston

OBJECTIVES
- To operate under the pressure of limited time
- To develop a problem-solving and decision-making process that can be transferred to work situations

Team Size
Any

Materials
Flight 287 to Boston Planning Sheet, Clues, and Solution (provided here, and available for download from virtualteambuildinggames.com)

Time
20 to 30 minutes

Technology
Conference call, online collaborative tool, or email

Procedure

This challenging logic puzzler will test your team's ability to solve a problem and reach consensus under pressure. Although achieving a perfect score is possible, the real value in this activity comes from exploring how teams operate when they have a hard-set deadline. Often in the performing stage of group development, a team experiences some conflict, or storming, as the deadline approaches. This game will raise a team's awareness and increase their skills when dealing with these common real-life issues.

1. Split larger teams into groups of four to six team members.
2. Post the planning sheet using the online collaborative tool or email the planning sheet to all the team members. Let the team(s) know that they will be under a tight time constraint to achieve the best score possible. They will

have 10 minutes to plan their strategy using the planning sheet as a guide, after which they will receive the clues. They can assign roles to make the process more manageable, develop a plan, discuss the technology they will use, and decide on other methods for solving the problem.

3. Once the teams have had a chance to plan, you can either post the clues using the online collaborative tool or email the clues to all the team members. At the end of another 10 minutes, the teams must submit their answers. Teams score 1 point for each answer, with a total possible score of 20 points.

Discussion Questions

1. How did you approach this challenge?
2. In what ways was the planning phase effective?
3. Did you stick to your plan? If not, how did your plan change?
4. What was sacrificed? As the deadline approached, what trade-offs were your team willing to make?
5. What are some reasons why plans change in real-life working situations?
6. How did the time constraint affect communication?
7. What did you learn?

GET IT ONLINE!

Flight 287 to Boston

Planning Sheet

Your team has 10 minutes to plan your strategy. You may assign roles to make the process more manageable, develop a plan, discuss the best technology to use, and decide on other methods for solving the problem.

Planning Information

Mateo, Julia, Donovan, Helena, and Pierre are colleagues on the same flight. Once they land, they will connect to other flights all over the world to visit clients. They have different types of luggage and like to pass the time in different ways. Using the clues that will be provided, your job is to figure out each person's destination and type of luggage, and what he or she is doing to pass the time.

GET IT ONLINE!

Flight 287 to Boston

Clues

The Toronto-bound traveler is carrying a silver briefcase.

The person listening to music does not own a black suitcase.

The person reading a book does not have a silver briefcase.

Helena is not reading a book.

Mateo is not playing solitaire.

The blue backpack owner is not playing solitaire.

The person heading to Singapore is not listening to music.

This will be Helena's first visit to Stockholm.

The person traveling to San Francisco carries a red duffel bag.

The person listening to music is not going to Sweden.

Pierre has a subscription to *National Geographic*.

The colleague with the Canadian client is not watching a movie.

The coworker heading to visit a client in the UK has a black suitcase.

Pierre is not leaving the United States.

Julia has a blue backpack.

The person connecting to the Toronto flight is not a reading a magazine.

Donovan is not going to San Francisco.

The person watching a movie carries a black suitcase.

The London traveler's name is not Mateo.

The Stockholm-bound colleague does not like the color blue.

Helena forgot her headphones, but doesn't need them for how she plans to pass the time on the long flight.

Mateo does not own a red duffel bag.

The person reading a magazine does not carry a purse.

GET IT ONLINE!

Flight 287 to Boston

Solution

Mateo, Toronto, silver briefcase, listening to music

Julia, Singapore, blue backpack, reading a book

Donovan, London, black suitcase, watching a movie

Helena, Stockholm, green purse, playing solitaire

Pierre, San Francisco, red duffel bag, reading a magazine

Lunch Is on Me

OBJECTIVES

- To show our appreciation to another team member
- To enjoy a good meal

Team Size

Any

Materials

None

Time

10 to 20 minutes for each team member over the course of a few weeks

Technology

Email

Procedure

Email each team member to provide him or her with the name of another person on the team. Sometime between receipt of the email and the next team meeting (or some other specified time period), each team member must surprise his or her partner by buying the partner lunch. This will require some undercover research as the team members figure out when the other person will be in the office to receive the lunch, what he or she likes to eat, what restaurants are nearby and can deliver, and so on. The map created in Map of Our Team (page 47) can provide useful hints regarding your partner's likes and dislikes and nearby restaurants.

Tips

Begin the next team meeting by asking, "So, what did you have for lunch?" Follow with the discussion questions.

Discussion Questions

1. How did you feel when you got your lunch?
2. How does it benefit us individually and as a team to be recognized?
3. What are some other ways we can recognize or show appreciation to others?

Magic Wand

OBJECTIVES

- To shift the team's focus from obstacles to possibilities
- To challenge limiting assumptions during your meeting or brainstorming session
- To increase the level of trust among team members

Team Size
Any

Materials
None

Time
20 minutes

Technology
Conference call

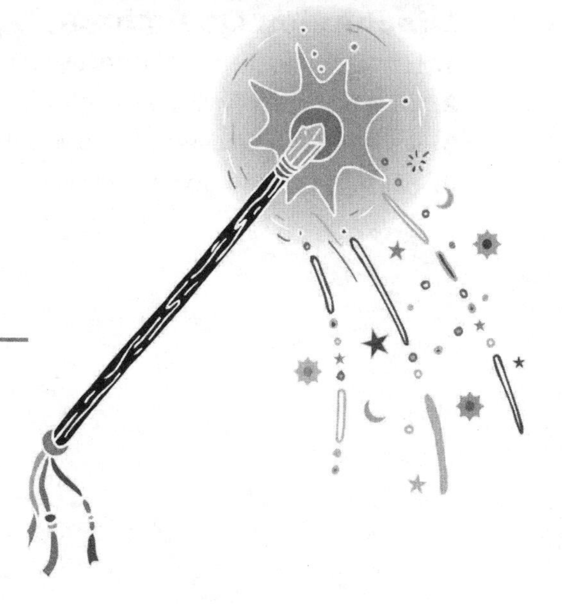

Procedure

What if your team had a magic wand it could wave to remove obstacles getting in the way of your project's success? How would you think differently about your project?

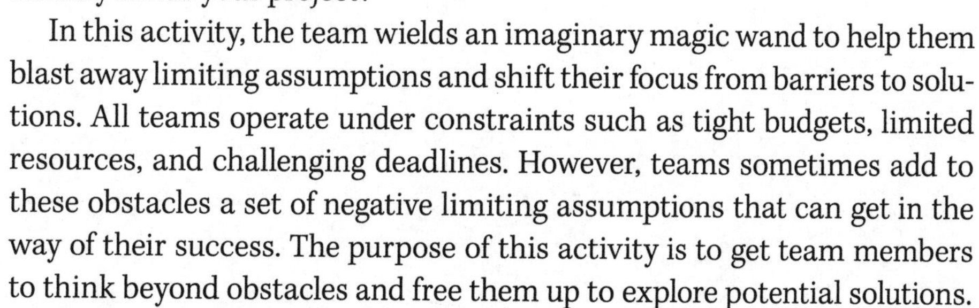

In this activity, the team wields an imaginary magic wand to help them blast away limiting assumptions and shift their focus from barriers to solutions. All teams operate under constraints such as tight budgets, limited resources, and challenging deadlines. However, teams sometimes add to these obstacles a set of negative limiting assumptions that can get in the way of their success. The purpose of this activity is to get team members to think beyond obstacles and free them up to explore potential solutions.

Tell the team they've been given an imaginary magic wand to use during this brainstorming session. One person at a time may wield the magic wand. If that person notices the team focusing on barriers, obstacles, or limitations at any point during the session, he or she can simply call out

"Zap!" (or another magic word of your choice). When the team hears "Zap!" they must immediately go from talking about barriers to talking about solutions. For example, if someone says, "We can't do that because it's over budget," another team member says, "Zap!" and the team must shift its focus to brainstorming about what *can* be done.

Pass the imaginary magic wand to several team members throughout your meeting. If they wish, have the team invent a magic word of their own to use in future meetings.

Discussion Questions

1. How often did team members use the magic wand?
2. What barriers or limiting assumptions did you blast with your magic wand?
3. If one of these barriers could really be removed, which one would it be?
4. What stops teams from removing barriers?

Project Spice Rack

OBJECTIVES

- To generate fresh ideas about your team's virtual work project
- To add depth to your team's brainstorming session

Team Size
Any

Materials
None

Time
25 to 30 minutes

Technology
Conference call, online collaborative tool

Procedure

1. Split large teams into at least three smaller brainstorming groups of two to four people.
2. Assign each group a spice from the Project Spice Rack below. The spices listed are suggestions; the game leader or the small groups are welcome to choose other spices not on this list.
   - Salt
   - Cinnamon
   - Pepper
   - Vanilla
   - Curry
   - Chile Powder
   - Allspice
   - Garlic
   - Mint
   - Wasabi
   - Saffron

3. Have each small group brainstorm about the qualities and characteristics of their spice via conference call, online collaborative tool, or both. For example, chile powder is strong, potentially overpowering, challenging for people who prefer mild flavors, but exciting for people with an adventurous palate.
4. After they have brainstormed, have each small group discuss ways to transfer the characteristics and qualities of their spice to their actual real-life work project.
5. Finally, in a whole-team conference call, have each spice group present their findings to everyone and invite further discussion to pick the spices (traits) that would add the right flavor to their real-life work project.

Tips

To help generate ideas about the spices, visit the Encyclopedia of Spices at theepicentre.com/Spices/spiceref.html.

Variations

You can use many themes for your brainstorming session. Some examples include fruits and vegetables, types of beverages, types of cars, and more. Your imagination is the only limit in this brainstorming exercise.

Discussion Questions

1. What ideas did your team generate in this exercise?
2. What blend of spices/traits is best for your project?

Reality Check

OBJECTIVES

- To perform a maintenance check on the team
- To provide a confidential way for team members to provide feedback

Team Size

Any

Materials

Reality Check Questionnaire (provided here, and available for download from virtualteambuildinggames.com)

Time

20 minutes

Technology

Conference call, email, team website or online collaborative tool

Procedure

We have provided many methods for gaining different perspectives of your project throughout the performing stage. This activity is to gain perspective of the team dynamics. During the performing stage, virtual teams often experience storming. Rather than wonder why you appear to be going backward through the stages, anticipate some "re-storming" as a natural part of the process. Use the Reality Check Questionnaire to assess how your team members are feeling or what their experience is regarding the overall workings of the team.

Email the questionnaire to all team members. Ask that they answer the questions and submit the questionnaire to you (the team leader) so you can compile the results. Post the results on the team website or using an online collaborative tool. During the next team meeting, have a debriefing discussion about this activity. Have the team brainstorm ways to work better together.

Tips

The team leader should facilitate this activity.

Discussion Questions

1. What can we do differently as a result of our reality check?
2. How can we ensure that we maintain healthy interpersonal relationships with others on our team?

GET IT ONLINE!

Reality Check Questionnaire

The team needs your honest assessment. Please take a few minutes to answer these questions about your experience on our team. After the team leader receives all the questionnaires, the information will be compiled and posted on the team website. Names will be kept confidential.

1. How do you feel we are doing overall? Where do we need to focus our attention?

2. How well are we working together? How could we be helping each other more?

3. What interpersonal issues have you experienced? What is the nature of these issues?

4. What problems, if any, do you see with our operating processes, communication, decision making, conflict-resolution methods, and use of technology?

Speed PassPhrase

OBJECTIVES

- To improve communication and creative problem-solving skills
- To explore ways to continuously improve a process
- To explore the concept of accountability

Team Size

6 to 12

Materials

A timer or stopwatch

Time

30 minutes

Technology

Conference call, online collaborative tool

Procedure

1. Have the group come up with a meaningful phrase that they will type collaboratively. The phrase can be a quote, a slogan, the lyrics to a song, or something else of their own invention. The phrase should consist of 20 to 30 words and can be more than one sentence in length. An example phrase is, "We are the best virtual team on Planet Earth. We boldly go where no team has gone before, and we do it with style!"
2. Once the team decides on a phrase, have them set a time goal for typing the phrase.
3. The team will have four attempts to type the phrase as quickly as possible to achieve their time goal.
4. After each attempt, the team may take up to five minutes to discuss ways to improve their result.

The team must adhere to the following rules:

- Every person on the team must type at least one word in the phrase.
- No one may type more than two consecutive words in a row.
- You may not use the delete key, the backspace key, or cut, copy, or paste.
- The team will incur a three-second penalty for:
  - Each typographical error
  - Two or more people accidentally typing at the same time

Allow five to ten minutes for the team to plan prior to their first attempt. When they are ready, start the team with "On your mark, get set, go!" When they finish typing the phrase, stop the timer and announce their time, making sure to add time for each penalty incurred by the team.

Give the team up to five minutes between each round to brainstorm ways to improve their score. If the team achieves its time goal before the fourth attempt, have them decide on a new, more challenging goal.

Discussion Questions

1. Was this challenge difficult for your team? Why or why not?
2. How did you organize yourselves to achieve your goal?
3. What changes did you make along the way in order to improve your result?
4. Did your team hold one another accountable? If so, how?
5. What did you learn from this activity that will be helpful to your virtual team?

Time Machine

OBJECTIVES
- To brainstorm ideas for project success
- To foster trust and communication

Team Size
Any

Materials
None

Time
15 to 20 minutes

Technology
Conference call, online meeting software (optional)

Today
Days ago
Weeks ago
The beginning

Procedure

This activity provides a safe way to discuss challenging topics related to project success and lessons learned.

Tell the team they have been given a time machine. This time machine will enable them to move backward through time, but only to one specific date. Once they arrive at the selected date, they may do one of three things:

1. Provide missing information
2. Provide a specific resource
3. Change a decision

Have the team brainstorm what date they would visit, what they would do once they were there, and what impact that would have on their current work. To help guide the brainstorming session, the facilitator or leader can ask the team the following questions:

- Was there a piece of missing information that turned out to be vital to the project?
- Was there a resource you did not use or have access to that would have made a difference?
- Was a decision made at the wrong time?

Once the team has discussed what they would go back and change, discuss what would be the impact of being able to make that change today. For example, would the project have been completed earlier, under budget, or have better met the client's requirements?

Conclude this activity by having team members look to the future. What will they change and how will they adjust their process on future virtual teams?

You can complete this process via a conference call or an online meeting. If using online meeting software, the facilitator will track the comments on the online whiteboard so each participant can see what has already been captured.

Discussion Questions

1. Why did you pick the date you did? What significance does it have?
2. What did you decide to do once you arrived at that date?
3. What would be the impact of that decision on our project today?
4. How can we implement these ideas into our projects in the future?

Walk the Plank

OBJECTIVES

- To increase levels of trust and build deeper connections among team members

Team Size

Up to 10

Materials

Walk the Plank graphics and fact sheet (available for download at virtualteambuildinggames.com)

Time

10 minutes

Technology

Online meeting software or online collaborative tool, conference call, email

Procedure

This activity provides a fun way to learn more about your team members. During an online meeting, the facilitator will show a slide with a pirate ship and a plank extending out over the ocean. A person is standing on the plank. By correctly answering questions about the team, team members can prevent this character from going into the water. For each correct answer, the person on the plank gets to stay put. For each incorrect answer, the person on the plank must move one step closer to the shark-infested waters.

Preparation: The facilitator emails the Walk the Plank fact sheet to each team member to complete and return. These facts will be turned into ten questions the facilitator will ask during the activity.

Next, the facilitator will upload the Walk the Plank graphics to your team's meeting software or online collaborative document. The graphics consist of a picture of a person standing on the plank of a pirate ship, which is sailing on shark-infested waters. There are a total of five pictures involved in this activity, each one with the same pirate ship and plank shown. The only thing that changes is the clip-art person who will move down the plank as the game progresses. The starting picture shows the person standing on the safe end of the plank. The other pictures depict various stages where the person is moving progressively down the plank and into the water.

Begin the game by showing the starting picture to the team. Ask the team ten questions from the fact sheets they submitted. When a team member answers a question correctly, the person on the plank remains standing; when the team answers a question wrong, the person moves one step closer to the shark-infested water. Four incorrect answers and the person ends up swimming with the sharks.

Discussion Questions

1. How did it feel when your team was able to save the person from going into the water?
2. If your person fell into the water, how did it feel?
3. How does our willingness to share personal information affect our virtual relationships?
4. What are the challenges to getting to know someone on a personal level when you are working virtually?
5. How can we overcome these challenges?

Yin and Yang

OBJECTIVES

- To understand how competition impacts team success
- To discover the benefits of a collaborative solution
- To build a high level of trust within the team

Team Size

Any

Materials

Yin and Yang Scoreboard (provided here, and available for download from virtualteambuildinggames.com). The scoreboard provided is for three groups; increase the number of columns if you have more groups playing.

Time

30 to 60 minutes

Technology

Conference call, online collaborative tool, text or instant messaging

Procedure

This game first appears to begin as a competition, but evolves into a collaborative activity. Teams will find value in recognizing what happens as they shift from a competitive mode to a cooperative one. The game itself is simple. For each round of play, groups decide whether to choose Yin or Yang. The scoring will depend on what all of the groups choose:

- If all of the groups choose Yang, each group scores 50.
- If exactly one group chooses Yin, that group scores 100 and all other groups score 0.
- If more than one group chooses Yin, all groups score 0.

1. Split the team into at least three groups of three to five team members. Groups do not have to have an equal number of people. Have the groups come up with a name to use on the scoreboard.
2. Have each group set up their own separate conference call to ensure privacy. Each group also needs a representative to communicate with you, the game's facilitator. The representative will communicate the team's decision with you through texting or instant messaging.
3. Tell the team: "The purpose of this game is to score as many points as possible. For each round, your group will discuss on your private conference call whether to choose Yin or Yang. When your group makes a decision, please have your group representative text or IM your choice to me."
4. Post the scoreboard using an online collaborative document so groups can see the results of each round.
5. Give the groups two to five minutes between rounds. As the rounds continue, you may need to give them more time, because some team members may begin to see the scoring benefit of working with the other groups and will need more time as they attempt to convince the rest of their group.
6. For each round, after you receive all of the groups' decisions, record the scores on the Yin and Yang Scoreboard. For example, if two groups choose Yin, all groups receive a score of 0. Groups will not see the specific group decisions unless a group is the only one to choose Yin and therefore receives 100 points.
7. If at any time someone asks you what the goal of the game is, respond by saying, "Your goal is to score as many points as possible." This sentence also appears at the top of the scoreboard as a reminder. Using this exact wording will become significant in the debriefing discussion.
8. Play enough rounds until the groups start to cooperate and then a few more rounds so they can score some points by doing so. What you usually find is that at least one group will start playing Yin almost immediately, and others will join in, so that by the end of the game, *no* team will have as many points as they would have if everyone had cooperated at the beginning and chosen Yang for every round.

Discussion Questions

1. How did you feel at the end of each round?
2. What was the most desirable outcome? What was the least desirable outcome?
3. Were any of you frustrated with your group's voting decisions? Why?
4. Did your strategy change along the way?
5. Was trust a factor? If so, in what way?
6. If your group chose Yang, why did your group decide to take a risk and trust that the other groups would follow?
7. What happened when the other groups did not react the way you hoped they would?
8. In what ways might competition lead to conflict?
9. How does competition affect the level of trust on a team?
10. How can we implement the lessons learned in this game to improve our team?

GET IT ONLINE!

Yin and Yang Scoreboard

Your goal is to score as many points as possible.

Scoring is as follows:

- If all groups choose Yang, each scores 50.
- If exactly one group chooses Yin, that group scores 100 and all other groups score 0.
- If more than one group chooses Yin, all teams score 0.

Round	Group "A"	Group "B"	Group "C"
1			
2			
3			
4			
5			
6			
7			
8			
9			
10			
Total			

5

Virtual Team-Building Games for the Transforming Stage

We keep moving forward, opening new doors, and doing new things because we're curious, and curiosity keeps leading us down new paths.

—Walt Disney

The Transforming Stage

This final stage brings closure. The team you have in this stage is a far different team than the one you started with. Developing a successful virtual team takes time, patience, and a willingness to rewrite the rule book. The relationships established on a virtual team are hard-earned and may continue long after the team disbands. Make sure you allow time for closure and reflection. As a leader, be ready with plenty of recognition and appreciation. Give team members ample time to recognize and appreciate each other, as well as their success.

Around-the-Clock Recognition

OBJECTIVES

- To provide recognition to the team members
- To celebrate the success of the team
- To foster a sense of accomplishment

Team Size
Any

Materials
Optional clock template (downloadable from virtualteambuildinggames.com)

Time
30 minutes

Technology
Online collaborative tool, conference call

Procedure

A handy way to keep track of who's who in your virtual meeting or conference call is to use the image of a clock face to indicate where people are "seated" at the virtual table. In this activity, your team members will go "around the clock" to honor and recognize the positive contributions made by each member of the team. This is a great activity to do when your team has completed a project or reached an important milestone.

Use the drawing feature from your online collaborative tool to create a circle representing the face of a clock. (You can also download a clock template from virtualteambuildinggames.com.) Write the name or paste a photo of each team member positioned around the face of the clock.

Identify the team member closest to one o'clock to be the first honoree. The rest of the team will express positive comments and offer recognition for the honoree's contribution to the team. Go around the clock one person at a time so that everyone gets to recognize the honoree. (Teams larger than six members may choose to save time by having just the three people to the honoree's right on the clock provide feedback.)

After a person has been honored, move on to the next honoree, working in a clockwise direction until all team members have been recognized.

Discussion Questions

1. Why is it important for team members to recognize each other's contributions?
2. What are some other ways to express appreciation for one another?

Caricature Match Game

OBJECTIVES

- A fun and creative way to discover how well we've come to know our teammates
- To showcase team members' creativity

Team Size
Any

Materials
Paper, pen

Time
10 to 15 minutes

Technology
Scanner, email, team website

Procedure

Have team members draw a picture to depict themselves without using any words—a picture that describes them in any creative manner. It can be a sketch of themselves, their hobbies, interests, family, or any and all of the above.

Have everyone scan their drawing and email it to the facilitator or game leader. After collecting the pictures, the leader can compile them and post them on the team website creating a "Team Self-Portrait Gallery." The goal is to see who can guess which drawing goes with which team member.

Discussion Questions

1. How well have we come to know each other?
2. What have we done over the course of our time together to build relationships?
3. How have our interpersonal relationships affected our team's success?

Variations

This can also be used in the team's beginning stages of group development as a way to get to know team members. For that version, use these questions for your debriefing discussion:

Discussion Questions for Variation

1. Why do we stick to "just the facts" when introducing ourselves to others?
2. How comfortable were you disclosing something other than the norm?
3. How might stretching our personal comfort zone help the team?
4. What are some other ways we can stretch our personal comfort zone?

I Hereby Recommend . . .

OBJECTIVES

- For team members to express appreciation for one another
- To write an endorsement for another team member
- To help build another's professional credibility

Team Size
Any

Materials
None

Time
10 to 20 minutes

Technology
LinkedIn

Procedure

As your team or project draws to an end, a great way to express appreciation for teammates is to compose a recommendation and post it to the LinkedIn profile of your colleague. Often people have the best intentions of doing this, but as time goes by, the opportunity is lost. This activity provides a designated time for everyone to do this.

A fun way to present this to your team is to announce, "We are going to start our meeting by taking a break, but this is a break with a purpose. The purpose is for you to take some time to write a recommendation for one or more of your teammates and post it to their LinkedIn profile. Your recommendations can be short but should be specific and sincere."

Some virtual teams work together on a continual basis, rather than being project driven. If that's the case with your team, we recommend doing this activity after the team reaches certain milestones.

Discussion Questions

No discussion questions are necessary.

Lessons Learned

OBJECTIVES

- To learn from the mistakes your virtual team made along the way
- To improve the process in future virtual teams we work on

Team Size

Any

Materials

None

Time

15 to 20 minutes

Technology

Email, conference call, online collaborative tool (optional), team website

Procedure

Because virtual teams don't have volumes of information to assist in their processes, in many cases, a virtual team will realize what works best in hindsight. As you bring your virtual team to an end, there are probably some things that team members wish they had known when the team first came together. This activity serves to bring closure and solidify what to do and what not to do as we work on future virtual teams. Prior to one of the team's final conference calls, send out an email requesting that team members take 10 minutes to jot down some lessons they had to learn the hard way while working on their virtual team.

Then, during the next team conference call, split the team into small groups of three or four. Have each small group, on their own conference call, come up with a list of "Lessons Learned" that combines all their individual ideas. After 10 minutes, bring your entire team together again via conference call to debrief. Assign one person to be a scribe for the team. The goal is to come up with relevant "Lessons Learned" to use when working on future virtual teams. Post the results on your team website or share by email.

Discussion Question

1. What was challenging about working virtually?
2. What were some obstacles that you did not anticipate?
3. How does the saying "You don't know what you don't know" apply to your experience with this team?
4. What would you do differently on future virtual teams?
5. What were some of the team's norms, rituals, and operating agreements that you would hope to re-create on future virtual teams?
6. What did you appreciate about this virtual team?
7. Looking at all the lessons we have learned collectively, which lesson was most relevant to you?

Word Cinquains

OBJECTIVES

- To reflect on the team's accomplishments
- To create a tangible takeaway
- To help bring a sense of closure

Team Size
Any

Materials
Word Cinquain Brainstorming Worksheet (provided here, and available for download from virtualteambuildinggames.com)

Time
20 to 30 minutes

Technology
Email, conference call, shared document or online collaborative tool, team website (optional)

Procedure

A cinquain is a type of poem. For this activity, team members will create a cinquain to encapsulate their time together. Incorporate this into one of your final team meetings. Prior to your meeting, split your team into groups of three or four people and email them the Word Cinquain Brainstorming Worksheet. Have each group set up a conference call to create a group cinquain using a shared document or online collaborative tool. At the beginning of the next meeting, have a representative from each group read their cinquain to the team. Invite team members to provide positive feedback and then take a few minutes for the discussion questions. Email a copy of all the poems to each team member or post the cinquains on your team website.

This activity normally leads to meaningful discussion about the most important aspects of team members' time together. By using the limited number of words, team members are forced to single out the most relevant and meaningful elements of their experience.

Tips

This is a great activity to use at your final team meeting or when you complete a significant project.

Variations

Have each team member create an individual cinquain before coming together to create a team cinquain.

Discussion Questions

1. What are some of your favorite team moments?
2. How can these cinquains help with your next virtual team?

GET IT ONLINE!

Word Cinquain Brainstorming Worksheet

A cinquain is a type of poem based on syllables. An alternate version of the cinquain poem, often called a word cinquain, is based on words instead of syllables. Word cinquains have the following pattern:

Line 1	one word—this is your title
Line 2	two words that describe your title
Line 3	three action words associated with the title
Line 4	four- or five-word phrase that relates to the title
Line 5	one word that is a similar word (synonym) for the title

Plan Your Cinquain

What is your topic? ______________________________

How would you describe your topic? What does your topic look like? Act like? Smell like? Taste like? Sound like? Feel like?

____

____

____

____

What can this (your topic) do (what action)?

____

____

GET IT ONLINE!

____

____

How do you feel about your topic?

____

____

____

What are some other words that have the same meaning as your topic (synonyms)?

____

____

____

____

About the Authors

Mary Scannell, founder of Biz Team Tools, is an elite trainer known for her engaging, high-energy style. For nearly two decades, Mary has developed and facilitated training programs on a wide variety of topics including communication, change management, conflict-to-collaboration, and customer service. Her clients include a long list of Fortune 500 companies and numerous small businesses across diverse industries.

Mary is the author of *The Big Book of Conflict-Resolution Games and The Big Book of Team-Motivating Games.* She is a member of the American Society for Training and Development and the Association for Experiential Education. She received a BS degree from the W. P. Carey School of Business at Arizona State University. Mary lives in Tempe, Arizona, with her husband, Kerry.

Mary's expertise in games and group activities extends through the full gamut of the topic from small classroom exercises to large-scale outdoor adventure events. She is an active member of her community, and for over a decade has worked with a local nonprofit to help Arizona youth become more connected to their schools, their homes, and their communities (EducationalEndeavors.com), through the use of experiential activities and ropes-course initiatives.

For more information or to schedule Mary Scannell to work with your team, please contact Biz Team Tools at 800–838–1535, or e-mail Mary at BizTeamTools.com.

Michael Abrams serves as Senior Director, Talent Optimization, at Banner Health. As part of the Talent and Organizational Effectiveness function, his team supports the organization through executive-, leadership-, and employee-development programs. Prior to his work at Banner Health, he held executive positions leading corporate training, software development, and e-commerce. He's been an active facilitator of executive and leadership development programs in the United States, Belgium, Germany, and the United Kingdom. Throughout his career he has successfully led and developed high-performing virtual teams. As a speaker, consultant, and workshop leader, he has helped many organizations implement innovative people-development programs that incorporate virtual collaboration. Michael's experience working with organizations in the health-care, financial, manufacturing, publishing, technology, and distribution industries provides a wealth of knowledge to apply to new projects. Michael holds both MBA and MEd degrees. Connect with Michael via Twitter (@mikeabrams), LinkedIn, or via his website, michaeltabrams.com.

Mike Mulvihill is the founder of PossibiliTEAMS, a team-building and training company offering fun and innovative team events to traditional corporate groups as well as virtual work teams around the globe. PossibiliTEAMS is the first company to offer a full lineup of team-building activities using virtual world technology. Mike has worked with teams throughout the United States, Europe, and Latin America, creating and facilitating team-building sessions for hundreds of organizations, ranging from Fortune 500 companies to small businesses, nonprofit groups, and government agencies. Some of the clients Mike has worked with include Liberty Mutual Insurance, Pearson Digital Learning, Bank of America, McKinsey & Company, Charles Schwab,

American Express, UPS, Motorola, Discover Financial Services, the Federal Highway Administration, and many more.

Mike is a member of the Society for Human Resource Management and the American Society for Training and Development. He received his bachelor's degree in organizational communication from Arizona State University. Connect with Mike at PossibiliTEAMS at 888–225–3610, or by email at Mike@PossibiliTEAMS.com.

Creativity Games
Epstein • $21.95

Humorous Training Games
Tamblyn/Weiss • $21.95

Motivation Games
Epstein/Rogers • $21.95

Leadership Games
Deming • $21.95

Six Sigma Training Games
Chen/Roth • $21.95

Team-Motivating Games
Scannell/Scannell • $24.95

Brain Building Games
Scannell/Burnett • $23.95

People Skills Games
Scannell/Rickenbacher • $24.95

Conflict Resolution Games
Scannell • $24.95